CourseBook Series

The CourseBook Series is the product of Dr. Mark H. Kavanaugh. Dr. Kavanaugh is a Professor of Psychology and Social Sciences at Kennebec Valley Community College. The CourseBooks contain the teaching content for each course.

Format

While definitively designed for digital distribution, each CourseBook is available in a number of formats. Distribution of the multi-touch ebook version is done exclusively through Apple Books. These CourseBooks may be purchased and downloaded directly to any iOS or Mac device.

Print versions of the CourseBooks are also available and are distributed through Amazon Kindle Unlimited.

Editing and Errors

Dr. Kavanaugh has written and edited all of this material but he is a horrible editor. He also cannot afford to have the work professionally reviewed. Mistakes, misspellings, broken links, and other errors may exist. Readers are encouraged to contact Dr. Kavanaugh directly to inform him of these errors for the next edition!

Copyright and Use

Dr. Kavanaugh owns the rights to the entire CourseBook. Others are free to use the CourseBook without permission. Graphics within the CourseBook are the original creations of Dr. Kavanaugh, downloaded from his Adobe Stock account, or are accompanied by attribution.

Index

How this CourseBook Works

The content of this CourseBook aligns with activities, expectations, and assignments that are found in the KVCC Learning Management System (LMS).

Students are expected to read and absorb the information in the CourseBook, read and review any textbook or other reading assignments, review the Assessment expectations outlined in each CourseBook Chapter, and participate in the expectations set by the instructor of the course in the LMS.

Chapter Organization

Each Chapter has been organized using an instructional design model called ALOTA, provides an outline of course materials that adheres to long-standing instructional design theory for adult learners. Namely, the model is greatly influenced by Gagne's Nine Events of Instruction

ALOTA

ALOTA is an acronym for the four essential parts of a lesson plan (or, in this case, chapter):

Attention
Learning Outcomes
Teaching
Assessment

Each Chapter in the CourseBooks series is organized in this manner in order to guide students through the material they are expected to learn.

Attention

Images, videos, text, and/or activities that bring readers into the focus of the lesson.

Learning Outcomes

Adhering to the language of Blooms Taxonomy of Learning Objectives, this section outlines the performance-based learning outcomes for the lesson. These align with the Assessment section of each lesson.

Teaching

This section can contain any variety of resources including text, lectures, recordings, videos, and links that provide a pathway through material to assist students in readying themselves for the Assessments.

Assessments

This section outlines assignments for students to demonstrate learning.

Additional Resources

Dr. K's Psychobabble

Dr. Kavanaugh also maintains a YouTube Channel called Dr. K's Psychobabble. You may find some of these videos embedded within this CourseBook.

Visit Dr. K's Psychobabble YouTube Channel

QR Codes

In order to ensure that readers of the print version of this CourseBook can still access online content, I have included QR Codes (such as the one listed here under my icon for Dr. K's Psychobabble.

Most smart phones are able to scan these codes with their camera and access the online material!

Apps in the CourseBook

Occasionally I will find mobile applications that relate to course content or are simply fun and engaging ways to learn. I will include links to these apps as the appear in the Apple App Store. It is likely that the same app is also available in Google Play but I will not usually provide the direct link to Google Play in the CourseBook.

Outcomes Alignment

Courses are designed to teach you a specific set of information and/or skills. These are largely determined by the specific learning outcomes through a course syllabus, in specific assignments and expectations, and in the structure of grading rubrics.

A course, however, often sits within a program that has learning outcomes associated with the expectations of external agents such as a licensing board, an accreditation body, and other agencies.

This section provides you with information on how the learning activities (assignments, discussions, quizzes, etc.) align with the learning outcomes as designated by the **American Psychological Associations** guidelines for undergraduate Psychology education and with the **American Association of Colleges and University's** (AAC&U) VALUE structure.

Alignment with the Guidelines From the American Psychological Association

The American Psychological Association (APA) produces guidelines for the development of curriculum in the teaching of Psychology at the undergraduate level.

Here is a direct link to the document

The CourseBook series is designed to outline instructional materials and activities for demonstrating competence and knowledge in Psychology in alignment with these guidelines.

This section of each Psychology CourseBook will outline the specific content and activities (assessments) that align with the APA expectations.

Knowledge Base in Psychology

Describe key concepts, principles, and over-arching themes in psychology.

- Chapter 1 Quiz - Goals of psychology
- Chapter 4 Quiz - Consciousness
- Chapter 5 Assignment - Gestalt
- Chapter 8 Discussion - Assimilation
- Chapter 9 Discussion A - Clocks
- Chapter 10 Quiz - Emotional intelligence

- Chapter 10 Quiz - Motivation

- Chapter 11 Discussion - Freud

- Chapter 15 Quiz - Abnormality

Develop a working knowledge of psychology's content domains.

- Chapter 5 Assignment - Gestalt

- Chapter 6 Discussion - Reinforcers

- Chapter 7 Discussion B - IQ

- Chapter 9 Discussion B - Erikson

- Chapter 9 Quiz - Generations

- Chapter 13 Discussion - Behavior Engineering

- Chapter 16 Quiz - Treatment vs. rehabilitation

- Chapter 16 Assignment - Mental illness

Describe applications of Psychology.

- Personal Change Special Assignment

- Chapter 4 Discussion B - Dreams

- Chapter 6 Assignment - Advertising

- Chapter 8 Discussion - Assimilation

- Chapter 8 Assignment - Study skills

- Chapter 10 Quiz - Emotional intelligence; achievement/motivation

- Chapter 11 Quiz - Big 5

- Chapter 12 Quiz - Roles and strain

- Chapter 12 Quiz - Social groups

- Chapter 12 Assignment - Looking glass self

- Chapter 14 Discussion - Stress

Scientific Inquiry and Critical Thinking

Use scientific reasoning to interpret psychological phenomena.

- Correlation Special Assignment

- Chapter 4 Discussion A - Sleep

Demonstrate psychology information literacy.

- Information Literacy Paper Special Assignment

- Chapter 7 Discussion A - Bias

- Chapter 16 Assignment - Mental illness

Engage in innovative and integrative thinking and problem solving.

- Chapter 14 Discussion - Stress

Interpret, design, and conduct basic psychological research.

- Chapter 2 Quiz - Describe research methods

Incorporate sociocultural factors in scientific inquiry.

- Chapter 5 Discussion - Culture

- Chapter 9 Quiz - Generations

- Chapter 10 Discussion - Anger

- Chapter 12 Discussion - Society

- Chapter 13 Quiz - Work culture

Ethical and Social Responsibility in a Diverse World

Apply ethical standards to evaluate psychological science and practice.

- Chapter 2 Discussion - Ethics

Build and enhance interpersonal relationships.

- N/A

Adopt values that build community at local, national, and global levels.

- N/A

Communication

Demonstrate effective writing for different purposes.

- Information Literacy Paper Special Assignment

- Chapter 1 Assignment - History

- Chapter 5 Assignment - Gestalt

- Chapter 6 Assignment - Advertising

- Chapter 8 Assignment - Study skills

- Chapter 12 Assignment - Looking glass self

Exhibit effective presentation skills for different purposes.

- **Chapter 16 Assignment - Mental Illness**

Interact effectively with others.

- All Discussions

Professional Development

Apply psychological content and skills to career goals.

- Chapter 1 Discussion - Careers

- **Chapter 8 Assignment - Study skills**

- Chapter 11 Quiz - Big 5

- Chapter 12 Quiz - Role and strain

- Chapter 13 Quiz - Work culture

Exhibit self-efficacy and self-regulation.

- **Personal Change Special Assignment**

- Chapter 8 Assignment - Study skills

- Chapter 10 Discussion - Anger

- Chapter 14 Discussion - Stress

Refine project management skills.

- **Chapter 8 Assignment - Study skills**

Enhance teamwork capacity.

- N/A

Develop meaningful professional direction for life after graduation.

- N/A

Alignment with the AAC&U VALUE Rubrics

In addition to the learning outcomes associated with the APA, specific to the field of psychology, the Department has adopted additional learning outcomes as present in the structure of the VALUE Rubrics produced by the Association of American Colleges & Universities (AAC&U).

VALUE stands for "value added learning for undergraduate education" and represents a national standard for the learning that should occur in undergraduate programs.

Below is a list of the specific expectations in this course that align with these outcomes.

Civic Engagement

- N/A

Creative Thinking

- Chapter 16 Assignment - Mental Illness

Critical Thinking

- Personal Change Special Assignment

Ethical Reasoning

- N/A

Global Learning

- N/A

Information Literacy

- Information Literacy Paper Special Assignment

Inquiry and Analysis

- Chapter 2 Quiz - Describe research methods

Integrative Learning

- Chapter 3 Discussion - Right-brain, Left-brain
- Chapter 6 Discussion -How reinforcement shapes our lives
- Chapter 9 Discussion A - Developmental Clocks
- Chapter 9 Discussion B - Generations
- Chapter 9 Quiz - Generations
- Chapter 10 Quiz - Emotional intelligence
- Chapter 10 Quiz - Motivation
- Chapter 12 Discussion - Society
- Chapter 12 Quiz - Roles and strain

- Chapter 12 Quiz - Social groups
- Chapter 12 Assignment - Looking glass self
- Chapter 13 Quiz - Work culture
- Chapter 14 Discussion - Personal Stress
- Personal Change Special Assignment

Intercultural Knowledge

- Chapter 5 Discussion - Culture
- Chapter 8 Discussion - Assimilation
- Chapter 12 Quiz - Roles and strain
- Chapter 12 Quiz - Social groups
- Chapter 13 Quiz - Work culture

Lifelong Learning

- N/A

Oral Communication

- Chapter 16 Assignment - Mental illness

Problem Solving

- Correlation and Decision Making Special Assignment
- Chapter 10 Discussion - Anger
- Personal Change Special Assignment

Quantitative Literacy

- Correlation Special Assignment

Reading

- Information Literacy Paper Special Assignment

Teamwork

- N/A

Written Communication

- Personal Change Special Assignment
- Information Literacy Paper Special Assignment
- Chapter 1 Assignment - History

- Chapter 5 Assignment - Gestalt
- Chapter 6 Assignment - Advertising
- Chapter 8 Assignment - Study Skills
- Chapter 12 Assignment - Looking glass self

Interpersonal Communication

- N/A

Introduction to Psychology

This CourseBook is an introduction and overview of the study of human behavior. Lectures and discussion topics will include motivation, perception, historical roots, biological bases of behavior, scientific methods, human development, psychopathology, and theory.

This CourseBook is designed to be used with a companion textbook.

Spielman, R.M., Jenkins, W.J., & Lovett, M.D. (2020). Introduction to Psychology (2nd Ed.). OpenStax.

Changes made to this Edition of the CourseBook

1. Statement regrading the sharing of personal information in any of the assessments has been added to the initial instructions for Assessments in Chapter 1.

2. New picture of the author.

3. General edits and clean-up.

About the Author

Mark H. Kavanaugh, Ph.D.

Mark Kavanaugh has been writing, teaching, and integrating technology into instruction for decades. He holds a Masters in Counseling, Masters in Instructional and Performance Technology, and a Ph.D. in Educational Psychology. Mark lives in Maine with his wife Katie.

Visit Mark's Website

An Introduction to Psychology

1

Attention

Crash Course in Psychology!

I really enjoy a series of videos on YouTube called CrashCourse Psychology.

The series is hosted by Hank Green (and sometimes by his brother John Green) and they produce funny and relevant videos about all sorts of topics.

I will be posting these videos here in the "Attention" section (and sometimes in other places as well). They are fast-paced, but you can always rewind and see them again and again!

Episode 1

INTRO TO PSYCHOLOGY

MOVIE - Introduction to Psychology

Psychology is Popular

There are many people interested in the field of psychology. We all have a mind and we all like to know how it works! According to an article in the Princeton Review, psychology is the 7th most popular major in the United States!

Of course there are a lot of myths associated with psychology as well. I took the opportunity to create a handout that describes both the myths and the amazing facts associated with psychology.

Myths of Psychology

Facts of Psychology

Learning Outcomes

Upon completion of this chapter, students should be able to:

1. Define psychology.

2. Provide examples of the goals of psychology.

3. Describe the influences of specific schools of thought in the history of psychology.

4. Discuss the diversity of interests and foci in the field of psychology.

Teaching

Note on Teaching: This section will describe all the material that you ned to review to complete the "Assessment" section successfully. While this section is akin to a "lecture" in class, not all the information you need to complete the assessments are contained in these pages. Other sources such as your textbook, online resources, movies, etc. may need to be reviewed.

The Study of the Soul

The origins of the word "psychology" is the "Scientific Study of the Soul" and it represents, even though the field itself is relatively new, one of the most ancient subjects of thought. For nearly all of history, people have been wondering why we do certain things, what motivates us to act, why are people different, and how do we think.

Penseur de Rodin's The Thinker

Although I do believe I have a bit of a bias, I think that the study of psychology is one of the most important sciences of all. Efforts to answer the previous questions have been impacting the world in tremendous ways. Psychology is all around us, and remarkably, we are all walking around with three pounds of the most complicated and fascinating object in the known universe, our brains.

A Definition of Psychology

The book simply states that psychology is the "scientific study of the mind." There is a lot to this definition though. I have often used the following definition of psychology (which you cannot use for your quiz!):

Psychology - The scientific study of human and animal behavior.

One of the reasons why I like my definition better is because I'm somewhat a behaviorist (more on that later!), but it covers pretty much the same thing as the book. Let's take the definition apart:

1. **Scientific** - this means that we use methodologies that are consistent and replicable.

2. **Study** - this is the disciplined practice of analyzing the results of our methods.

3. **Human and Animal** - modern and historical models of psychology are full of work done with both humans and animals.

4. **Behavior** - the focus, as a science, is on observable phenomenon, or the implicit observable results of unobserved behavior (you can't watch someone and know they are reading, but you can test them on the content and discover if it is likely they were reading).

The Scientific Method

One of the primary models by which psychologists conduct their work is by applying the scientific method. The scientific method provides a structure and discipline that manages the behavior of the researcher and provides consumers of the information a degree of confidence in the results. We will go into this much deeper in Chapter 2.

Goals of Psychology

Throughout history, the goals of psychology have been fairly consistent.

1. **Describe** human and animal behavior - from this goal we attain our exacting terminology. Much of psychology is learning the terminology and exact language we use to describe things.

2. **Explain** human and animal behavior - from this goal we generate theories and models that explain the relationships between factors. We might have theories that explain what motivates us to behave and we may have other theories that describe the relationship between the amount of time you study and your grades. Either way, they are all theories and they are all trying to explain behavior.

3. **Predict** human and animal behavior - with the knowledge that comes from theories we can sometimes predict behavior. For instance, if there is a natural disaster in the area, there are formulas based on population, demographics, and the nature of the disaster, that can predict

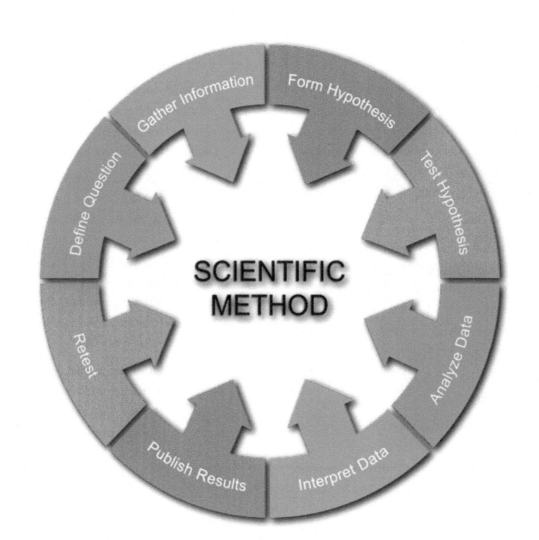

how many counselors will be needed to provide support services to survivors.

4. **Control** human and animal behavior - ultimately with good and accurate models of behavior we can exhibit some control over behavior. For instance, if we know that providing outlines of material discussed in class increases test scores, we can purposefully provide these outlines to our students.

The quest for scientific understanding of the human experience rests on the exploration of these four goals. Let's look at an example:

Let's say that you are a psychologist working for NASA in their preparation to send people to Mars. You know it is going to be a long trip for those individuals. It is also going to be in cramped quarters. You are concerned about long-term mental health care for the astronauts. So let's set some goals.

*First, you want to **describe** the situation in which the people will be living and the measures of mental health you are going to*

use. You create an exact model of the spacecraft that will be going to Mars and decide that you are going to use a number of clinical measures of mental health including depression scales, anxiety scales, critical thinking tests, stress tests, etc. We have defined the situation and the measures of the behavior.

*We then move on to **explain** the relationship between the variables. We ask our question: How does long-term habitation in the spacecraft impact the values on all these tests? We place volunteers into the craft and measure changes in values over time.*

*From this step we formulate **theories** that tie together variables such as living in cramped quarters with measures such as depression. With these theories we can now make **predictions**. According to our data, our astronauts are likely to experience an increase in depression and anxiety over the course of their trip. Even though our test subjects actually did not go to Mars, we predict that our astronauts will experience some of the same impacts.*

*Finally, our goal is to keep our astronauts as healthy and happy as possible for their trip. We want to **control** this as much as*

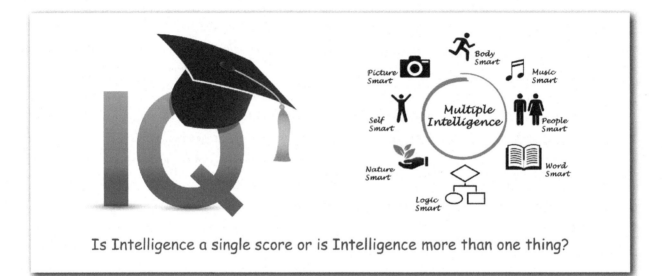

Is Intelligence a single score or is Intelligence more than one thing?

There are a lot of ways to describe "intelligence"

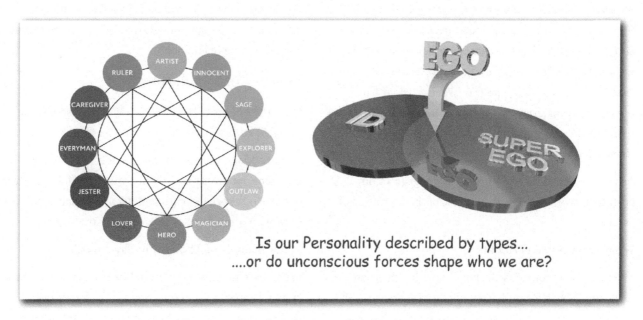

Is our Personality described by types...
....or do unconscious forces shape who we are?

There are also a lot of ways to describe "personality"

possible. *Knowing that they are likely to experience increased depression and anxiety, we design activities for the astronauts to engage in that are known to decrease depression symptoms. We might enlist the help of a ground-based psychologist to talk with the astronauts daily through the trip. We might ensure that our selected astronauts do not already have a predisposition for depression and/or anxiety, and finally, we may ensure a good supply of anti-depressants and anti-anxiety medication on the craft!*

As you can see in this example, psychologists accomplish their work through the pursuit of the four goals of psychology!

What this Course is About

The rest of this course is all about exploring the theories that we have for understanding human and animal behavior which enable us to describe, explain, predict, and sometimes control behavior.

However, unlike other sciences, psychology is very complex, and the factors that lead to human behavior are often unknown (i.e. the theories are incomplete).

So, in this course you will be exposed to a number of different theories and models that might attempt to explain the same phenomenon!

History of Psychology

Since the origins of psychology are in philosophy, the actual history of psychology is as old as thinking.

The textbook outlines various major schools of thought that appeared over the early history of psychology. Each of these is associated with famous individuals who were creators of the school or influential in the school.

Major Schools of Thought in Psychology

When psychology was first established as a science separate from biology and philosophy, the debate over how to describe and explain the human mind and behavior began. The first school of thought, structuralism, was advocated by the founder of the first psychology lab,

Wilhelm Wundt.

Almost immediately, other theories began to emerge and vie for dominance in psychology. The following are some of the major schools of thought that have influenced our knowledge and understanding of psychology:

Wilhelm Wundt

Structuralism vs. Functionalism

Structuralism was the first school of psychology, and focused on breaking down mental processes into the most basic components. Major structuralist thinkers include Wilhelm Wundt and Edward Titchener.

Functionalism formed as a reaction to the theories of the structuralist school of thought and was heavily influenced by the work of William James. Major functionalist thinkers included John Dewey and Harvey Carr.

Behaviorism

John B. Watson

Behaviorism became the dominant school of thought during the 1950s. Based upon the work of thinkers such as John B. Watson, Ivan Pavlov, and B. F. Skinner, behaviorism holds that all behavior can be explained by environmental causes, rather than by internal forces.

Behaviorism is focused on observable behavior. Theories of learning including classical conditioning and operant conditioning were the focus of a great deal of research.

B.F. Skinner

Psychoanalysis

Sigmund Freud

Sigmund Freud was the founder of the psychodynamic approach. This school of thought emphasizes the influence of the unconscious mind on behavior. Freud believed that the human mind was composed of three elements: the id, the ego, and the superego.

Erik Erikson

Other major psychodynamic thinkers include Anna Freud, Carl Jung, and Erik Erikson.

Humanistic Psychology

Humanistic psychology developed as a response to psychoanalysis and behaviorism. Humanistic psychology instead focused on individual free will, personal growth, and self-actualization. Major humanist thinkers included Abraham Maslow and Carl Rogers.

Carl Rogers

Gestalt Psychology

Gestalt psychology is based upon the idea that we experience things as unified wholes. This approach to psychology began in Germany and Austria during the late 19th century in response to the molecular approach of structuralism. Rather that breaking down thoughts and behavior to their smallest element, the gestalt psychologists believed that you must look at the whole of experience. According to the gestalt thinkers, the whole is greater than the sum of its parts.

Cognitive Psychology

Jean Piaget

Cognitive psychology is the branch of psychology that studies mental processes including how people think, perceive, remember, and learn. As part of the larger field of cognitive science, this branch of psychology is related to other disciplines including neuroscience, philosophy, and linguistics.

One of the most influential theories from this school of thought was the stages of cognitive development theory proposed by Jean Piaget.

All the images in this section are from Wikipedia.

The Current field of Psychology

What do you think about when you hear that someone is a psychologist? Most people would say that a psychologist is a person who engages people in therapy and helps them solve problems. You would be right, for most psychologists, but not all.

The field of psychology is one that has interests, and conducts research, in nearly every aspect of the human experience! One great way to get a feel for how many different focal areas are covered by psychology is to visit the website of the American Psychological Association (APA).

The APA is the largest organization representing psychologists in the world. The organization is divided into 54 divisions that reflect the diversity of interests of psychologists around the world.

Visit the APA website and explore the 54 Divisions!

Another great organization is the Association of Psychological Science.

Visit the APS website!

Assessment

This section describes the activities and assignments associated with this chapter. Be sure to check with your instructor as to which ones you are expected to complete.

Privacy

Many of the assessments (Discussions, Quizzes, and Assignments) ask you to engage in self-exploration and self-disclosure. Often the best way to understand concepts in the field is to apply them to our experiences.

Although the expectation of the class is that any information you share about yourself will be respected and confidential, you may not wish to disclose certain aspects of your personal life. In these instances you can either elect to not participate in the assessment (resulting in a zero grade), fabricate a story, or use another person (without sharing identifying information) to complete the assessment.

Discussions

These activities are primarily geared toward students who are taking the course in either an online or hybrid format. It is expected that students will post an answer to the prompt and reply to at least two other students' posts in order to obtain full credit for the discussion. All posts must be substantive and contribute to the discussion.

Quizzes

Quizzes ask students to reflect on specific course concepts and answer exploratory questions, provide examples, definitions, and at times, express their knowledge with multiple-choice and/or matching type questions.

Assignments

These activities entail the creation of a "document" of sorts that needs to be sent to your instructor. Most of these are papers. All papers must be submitted to the identified "drop box" for the assignment and must be in either Microsoft Word or PDF format.

Pay attention to expectations such as title page and APA formatting if these are indicated in the instructions.

Other assignments may entail different types of "documents" including presentations, artwork, charts, spreadsheets, and/or movies. Instructions on how to submit these will be included in their descriptions.

Though they will not be repeated, all of the above notes should be assumed in subsequent chapters, unless otherwise indicated.

Chapter 1 Discussion - Careers

Review the different career options for people with a degree in psychology on the APA website. Reflect on at least two areas that were a surprise to you or new to you. Do any of these ideas appeal to you as a potential career?

Chapter 1 Quiz

1. Consider the four goals of psychology (define, explain, predict, and control). Provide an exam-

ple of a specific psychological problem and how the field achieves these goals.

Chapter 1 Assignment - History

Purpose

The purpose of this assignment is to explore the history and influence of a specific individual from the history of psychology. In the present, we are often unaware that ideas that seem new have usually had roots in the distant past. By exploring the contributions of individual psychologists we can appreciate the link between the current thinking in the field and its origins.

Skills and Knowledge

You will demonstrate the following skills and knowledge by completing this assignment:

1. Identify a key individual from the history of psychology.

2. Develop research skills to find the education, experiences, work, publications, and personal life of a person.

3. Construct a resume formatted review of an individual from the history of psychology

4. Upload the paper to the appropriate assignment dropbox.

Task

There is a rich resource of the history of psychology and the individuals who created this history readily available on the web. We are going to be using a great resource for this kind of research in this assignment, Wikipedia!

Review this content and find a single individual that you are interested in learning more about. There are many to choose from but their names are not listed, they are in the context of the narrative on this site.

Names that are highlighted on this page have their own Wikipedia page and you can use the page of your selected person to complete this assignment.

Here is the page in Wikipedia on the History of Psychology.

History of Psychology

Imagine that this person is seeking a job teaching in the Department of Social Sciences and Psychology at KVCC. Construct a cover letter and resume of this person based on the information contained in the Wikipedia page.

The cover letter and resume will need to contain specific elements as listed in the rubric below. Keep in mind that this is all supposed to be submitted as a single document. The first page of your document is the Cover Letter with the Resume starting on page 2.

Criteria for Success

Use the rubric below as a guide to this assignment.

Cover Letter   20 points

Page 1 of your document should be your cover letter. The letter should be addressed to your professor. Your cover letter should highlight aspects of the person's career that are related to teaching and be convincing in terms appealing to your professor to hire them for the job.

Resume Design   20 points

The resume itself should be very professionally laid out with bold sections that make it easy to read and understand the qualifications of the individual.

Resume Content   30 points

The following sections should be included in the body of the resume.

- Name and Contact Information (for this use the place where the person last lived)
- Picture of the individual.
- Education (bullet points)
- Publications and Presentations (bullet points)

- Work History (bullet points)

- 1 paragraph summary of major contributions to psychology.

Personal History   20 points

Summary essay of life events including birth date, place of birth, major family members, marital history, children, places they have lived.

Mechanics   10 points

Spelling, syntax, and organizational structure of the paper. Clear and organized. The cover letter and resume should be elegant and professional in presentation.

To assist you in this process, I have found a site that provides a number of resources related to writing and formatting a professional cover letter and resume.

ResumeGenius

On this site, review the link titled "Resources" and you will find Cover Letter and Resume guidelines, examples, and templates.

MS Word has a number of Cover Letter and Resume templates so you can make a great presentation.

Psychological
Research

Attention

COVID-19 and Psychology

The challenges associated with the global COVID pandemic have provided the field of psychology with an opportunity to study human behavior in a way that could not have happened any other way.

The Biggest Psychological Experiment in History is Running Now

Learning Outcomes

Upon completion of this chapter, students should be able to:

1. Explain how scientific research is important to understanding behavior.

2. Identity acceptable methods that could be used to answer a psychological question.

3. Demonstrate the use of statistical analysis in decision making.

4. Identity ethical issues with particular approaches to research with humans.

Teaching

Why get scientific?

Part of the answer to this question lays in the history of psychology. Prior to the modern age, most of what we call psychology was in the field of philosophy, with no specific methods other than deep thinking. While these methods produced profound knowledge and thoughts (consider the early thinking of the Greeks and Ancient Chinese cultures) they placed psychology on the track to having difficultly legitimizing itself.

In the days of early psychology, colleges and universities were filled with scientists who studied chemistry, physics, biology, engineering, and many other fields. With the early psychologists relegated to the philosophy departments, they wanted more. It is at this point that they decided to embrace the methodologies used by their more prestigious (and higher paid!) colleagues in the other sciences. They adopted the "scientific method."

Episode 2
RESEARCH & EXPERIMENTATION

MOVIE - Psychological Research

The Scientific Method

The scientific method is what made psychology a science. Its practices and disciplines began to act in accord with the same principles that had governed the other sciences.

The main benefit of this approach to studying human beings is that it attempts to make something that is often very subjective (feelings, motivation, learning, etc.) measurable and objective and easier to analyze.

This creates limits on what the field can actually study. Just as in the field of physics, there are ideas that we are able to test with the tools and understanding we have today, while other theories lay outside of our current reach. Consider that the field of psychology gladly studies how young children learn, but they are less enthusiastic about the study of ESP (extrasensory perception). If, indeed, powers of the mind such as ESP do exist, they are currently beyond the scope of the research methods of psychology (thus the research that DOES happen in this area is largely outside of mainstream psychology).

Advantages of the Scientific Method

The benefits of using this methodology are as follows:

1. Clear and standardized language to describe the elements of the research

2. Clear process of defining and gathering the data needed

3. Clear identification of the goals of the research and its hypotheses

4. Clear procedures for analyzing and interpreting data

5. Accountability to peers on all aspects of the research

6. Research can be accurately replicated to check the results

Why Psychology is a DIFFICULT Science

As we discussed in Chapter 1, one of the greatest challenges to the science of psychology is that the results it produces are largely not definitive. While we understand such things as the impact of abuse and how too much alcohol changes brain chemistry, we are left with only theories as to why someone becomes an abuser or why some people can drink a lot and never become alcoholics.

The reason for this relatively grey-colored set of results is because, in psychology, there are usually many causes or factors associated with a phenomena. Because there are many factors that play into a situation, we are less able to accurately predict events and more able to predict the PROBABILITY of an event. We will get into statistical analysis a bit later.

Let's look at the example of abuse, specifically spousal abuse.

What causes Spousal Abuse?

We may be tempted to say that persons who abuse their spouses are just jerks, but in order to address these horrible situations, we are going to have to know more about the abuser and their targets.

A brief review on the website PsychCentral reveals a number of factors that contribute to the instance of spousal abuse:

1. Need to control and dominate the partner

2. Low self-esteem

3. Perceptions regarding women and their role

4. Difficulty regulating anger and other emotions

5. This was the norm in their family

In addition to this, there are social factors that may contribute to these instances as well:

1. "Macho" image of manhood in the media

2. Portrayal of violence for problem resolution

3. Peer influences and status as men and women

4. Sociocultural expectations of men and women's roles in the family

5. A lack of consequence to the perpetrator due to low reporting by victims

6. Unemployment

The science of psychology that has been applied to this particular question has revealed that there is no one real reason why this happens. Each of these factors can play a role in any instance of spousal abuse and many interact with each other to produce the "perfect storm" in which the abuse begins.

This is frustrating for many people who begin to study psychology and come to realize that while psychology addresses many of the most vital questions of our existence and our survival, we often come up with many, and sometimes contradicting answers!

Research Methodology

So, what would you do if you really wanted to find out about the factors associated with abuse? Let's use this as a launching pad for an examination of the different methods used by psychologists to answer these questions.

Clinical or Case Study

This method attempts to answer questions by looking at a single example. The example could be a person, or a family, or a business, or even a country...the point is we are looking at ONE example and answering the question for that example.

Lots of the world of psychology is based on case studies, and while they provide a lot of detailed information, the results are not easily generalizable to other people. That means that we can't assume we know the answer to the question for OTHER people aside from our case study.

For our research on abuse, we may find a family wishing to participate in interviews, questionnaires, and an examination of records. From this data would would determine what the factors were in that particular situation.

Naturalistic Observation

This method has the researcher enter the environment in which the phenomena is taking place and observe the behavior directly. They may make more observations than you get from a case study and there will be an opportunity to learn much more about environmental impacts on the situation.

The drawback for this method is that if the people know they are being observed, they may act differently. Think about how you might act when the boss is around as opposed to when they are not!

For our research on abuse, we will probably not be able (nor want to) make observations directly of the abuse itself. However, we could attend a support group of either abusers or victims and listen in on what they tell us. Conversely we could observe identified abusers in other environments to see if they have tendencies to over-control, or low self-esteem, and explore those factors.

Surveys (and Tests/Instruments)

It would be difficult to find someone who has not competed a survey! This method allows us to ask a series of questions to individuals and explore their thoughts and opinions on the subject. The real advantage of this particular method is that it is easy to administer, it often allows for anonymous participation, and it is less expensive and time consuming.

The drawbacks to this method include:

1. Poor question design (leading questions, unclear questions)

2. Fabricated answers by participants

3. Poor return rate (not everyone wants to do the survey)

4. Characteristics of people who answer surveys (there may be a difference between those who would participate in a survey and those who would not)

For our research on abuse, we could construct a survey that asks abusers and thier victims about the factors we want to explore. We could do this online and anonymously and potentially collect lots of data. We could also easily distribute the survey to shelters and other places where we may locate this population.

Archival Research

This method examines existing current and historical records and draws conclusions based on the factors identified in those records. One great aspect of this type of research is that it does not need to involve any people (except for the researchers). Once you have access to the records, they remain accessible and available for as long as you want (usually).

The drawbacks to this method include the fact that not all historical records are complete or accurate. Often there is no way to adjust for this. In addition, some records are difficult to acquire.

For our research on abuse we could examine the clinical records of abusers and victims, look at ER records, etc. Specific to one of our models that explain abuse, we might do this type of study in an area where a major employer went out of business, measure the reported incidents of abuse before and after, and speculate the impact unemployment had on the rate of occurrence.

Longitudinal and Cross-Sectional

HARVARD

SECOND GENERATION

STUDY

Check out the **Harvard Study of Adult Development** that has been going on for over 80 years and is now looking at the second generation of participants!

These two methods are useful when you are asking how a phenomena changes over the life of a person. Longi-

tudinal research looks at an individual or group over time and measures how the phenomena changes, while cross-sectional research looks at different groups at different ages all at the same time (one group that is age 5, another group at age 10, etc.).

The drawback to these methods is that they are usually time and effort intensive, particularly the longitudinal study.

For our research on abuse, we could follow families that have experienced abuse over time to see how patterns persist or how those families break out of the abuse cycle. We could also interview families at periods of time post-intervention to see how effective the interventions have been over time.

Experiments

Probably the most famous of the methods is the experiment. Experiments are popular and useful because they allow researchers to pinpoint specific aspects of a complex phenomenon and test hypotheses about these relationships. Experiments are usually set up as mock situations where subjects are asked to complete tasks. As many of the variables (factors) associated with the phenomenon are controlled by the researcher, the results often give insight into the relationship between one factor and another.

One famous experiment in the history of psychology was the Obedience Study conducted by Stanley Milgram. This experiment attempted to see how people would behave under the influence of an authority figure. Watch the video to get a sense of this study.

The drawbacks of experiments include the following:

1. The contrived situation is not like the "real world."

2. Not all other variables can be controlled.

3. There are risks associated with doing some kinds of experiments with human subjects.

For our study on abuse, we might examine how a subject reacts (behaviorally and physically) when they are put into challenging

situations. If, for example, the need to control is a part of the abuse struggle, we could contrive situations in which our subjects' control is challenged to see how they react.

Early studies in the field of experimental psychology with human subjects, like the Milgram study, were controversial to say the least. These studies led the American Psychological Association and the National Institute of Health (NIH) to create ethical codes for experiments involving human beings. While we have learned a lot from studies like Milgram's, it would be difficult to replicate a study like his because of these rules.

NIH Guiding Principles for Ethical Research

Essentially, these guidelines outline that studies with human subjects should:

1. ...have a social and clinical value.

2. ...be conducted to ensure scientific validity.

3. ...engage practices that select subjects fairly.

4. ...have a favorable risk to benefit ratio.

5. ...be subjected to an external review.

6. ...allow for informed consent on the part of the subjects.

7. ...be respectful for potential and enrolled subjects.

The 25 Most Influential Psychological Experiments in History

The 20 Most Unethical Experiments in Psychology

Scientific Design and Decision Making

A lot of the knowledge base of psychology was constructed using the variety of methods that are previously mentioned. Through these processes, researchers engaged in the steps of the scientific method and reached conclusions about the data they collected. Here we are going to look at how they come to these conclusions.

First we need to revisit the scientific method itself.

I'm going to use the following example to teach you about how to conduct a **quantitative** scientific study. The "quantitative" part means that we are going to be

MILGRAM SHOCK STUDY

MOVIE - Obedience Study by Stanley Milgram

collected numerical data and conducting statistical analysis of this data. The other type of research, **qualitative**, will be described after.

Define Question

Tools like Keynote and PowerPoint are used in many settings... but are they effective teaching tools or colorful distractions?

In all of my classes, I utilize the computer application Keynote (this is Apple's presentation software and is like Microsoft PowerPoint).

These take some effort and I use them to guide my lecture, but I wonder if they are also helpful to my students. So, I want to pose a question:

What is the effect of in-class slide presentations on students' retention of course material?

Gather Information

The next step in the process is to gather information. This does NOT mean that we start asking students how they feel about my presentations, this is where we turn to the scientific literature and see what we ALREADY KNOW about the effect of slides on learning.

We do this in order to:

1. Find out if our study has usefulness and meaning.

2. Find out if our study has already been done.

3. Find out if our study is different from what has already been done.

4. Find out more about how to define our variables.

5. Find out how to design our study.

6. Find existing theories that might support our hypotheses.

In this process, often referred to as the **literature review**, I would need to conduct an exhaustive search of the professional journals in psychology for articles that have already been written about this topic.

I would limit my search to professional journals because I'm only interested in **peer-reviewed** studies, not what you find on the internet!

Related to my study, I did a search and found this article. This is a good article because it is actually a **meta-analysis,** a statistical analysis of a bunch of other articles, combined into one study!

Baker, J.P., Goodboy, A.K., Bowman, N.D., & Wright, A.A. (2018). Does teaching with PowerPoint increase students' learning? A meta-analysis. *Computers & Education, 126*, 376-387.

Here is the abstract to this article:

PowerPoint has become a ubiquitous tool for instructors who teach college students. Almost two decades of student learning research has examined the impact of traditional instruction (i.e., chalk and talk) versus instruction aided by PowerPoint. This research has revealed inconsistent and contrasting results. To probe this inconsistency, a meta-analysis of 48 studies was conducted to determine if students learn more when taught the same material using PowerPoint compared to traditional instruction. Results revealed that on average, there was no difference in students' learning based on the type of instruction they received (Hedges' g=0.067; 95% CI: −0.103 to 0.236). Moderation analyses revealed that the sampling frame, such as a focus on K-12 versus college students, explained heterogeneity in the findings. Specifically, K-12 students' cognitive learning increased as a result of PowerPoint instruction, but this effect did not emerge for college students. The results of this meta-analysis suggest that researchers should move past strictly comparing the absence or presence of this instructional tool, to instead examine how instructors are integrating features of PowerPoint in ways that help students learn.

Notice that the author is suggesting that we don't conduct a simple experiment to answer this question, but we will design one anyway!

Once we have a whole bunch of these articles and we have reviewed them all, we are ready to start designing our study!

Form Hypothesis

An hypothesis is an educated guess based on the evidence that you have found in the peer-reviewed literature. We want to predict what is going to happen in our study. We may be trying to support an existing theory or we may be introducing new variables to modify the theory in our study...either way, we want to make predictions as to what we think will happen.

To do this, we will need to take three steps:

1. Define our variables (very precisely)

Variables are the factors we are trying to explore. We are often looking to see if there is a **relationship** between variables. There are two general types of relationships...correlations and cause-effect. We will talk about correlations later.

In cause-effect relationships there are two types of variables...there is the variable that causes something to happen (independent variable) and the variable that is changed by the cause (dependent variable).

In our current example, the slide presentation is the independent variable (IV) and the degree of learning is the dependent variable (DV). Our study is trying to determine if the IV produces a change in the DV...does having slide presentations impact grades.

We need to decide how we are going to define different parts of our question. Namely we need to define "effect," the nature of the "slide presentation," and a measure for "learning."

To this end, let's suggest the following: We are going to define the "slide presentation" as my slideshow on Chapter 2 in Introduction to Psychology. The "learning" is going to be measured by a 20 question quiz at the end of class, and the "effect" will be measured by different scores on this quiz.

2. Define our experimental hypothesis (what we think will happen)

Now, according to the study I cited above, whether I expose students to the slide show or not should have no impact on learning. My hypothesis would be stated like this.

"There will be no differences between the quiz scores of students who were exposed to the class slide show and those who were not."

3. Define our NULL hypothesis (what we think will NOT happen)

The null hypothesis simply states what would be true if we did not support the experimental hypothesis.

"There will be a difference between the quiz scores of students who were exposed to the class slide show and those who were not."

Test Hypothesis

Now comes the fun part! To do this study I've decided that I'm going to split my class into two groups (randomly assigned) and teach one group the material on Chapter 2 using my slide show and teach the other group the material on Chapter 2 without my slide show.

At the end of each class I will have students complete the quiz and collect those results. There are all kinds of things wrong with this design (can you think of any?), but we will go with it anyway!

Analyze Data

Now that I have collected all the test scores I could average the scores in each group and compare the groups. Let's say the average of Group 1 (with slide show) was 87 and the average of Group 2 (without slide show) was 85, I could conduct a number of different statistical tests to see if this was a "significant" enough difference to warrant an effect. For now, let's assume that it was not, so we are ready to interpret the data.

Interpret Data

Our interpretations always include two things: decision making regarding our hypotheses and a description and speculation on the limits of the study. Here is a summary of my interpretation of these results:

The data collected in our study supports our hypothesis that there was no difference in mean scores between groups on the class quiz. This is consistent with the literature on the effect of class slide shows on learning. These results, however, are limited in generalizability by a number of factors. First, the class size was small and as such, the comparison groups were very small.

This limits the statistical power of the results. In addition, one class (the one with the slide show) was conducted prior to the second class (the one without the slide show.) This sequencing of the material created the situation where the groups experienced the class at different times of the day and each class may have been taught slightly differently as a result of instructional practice.

Publish Results

Now we want to share our study with others who might be interested in knowing about what we did. We can attempt to write this up and submit it for publishing in a journal or we can distribute it to colleagues and/or post it on the web. This opens the whole study up to analysis and critique from others. Yikes!

Retest

At this point, upon receiving ample peer critique, we may decide to re-do our study and take into consideration some of the feedback we got from peers and the limitations of the study outlined previously. The

MOVIE - Scholarly vs Popular Periodicals

Sometimes the Peer-Review process can be daunting!

process of research is cyclical and continues on and on, particularly in the grey world of psychology!

Quantitative Research and Statistics

The study that I just described is considered quantitative research because it has to do with variables that can be measured with numbers. Although "class type," with or without slide show, is not such a variable, the quiz scores were.

Previously, I mentioned the limitation of "significance" and this is where statistics comes in. Statistics is a form of math that is used to determine the relationship between variables. At least one of the variables needs to be numerical in order for it to work. Statistical procedures are used in order to address the following questions:

1. Is there a difference?

2. In what direction is the difference?

3. Is the difference large, small, and/or significant?

4. How does the size of the groups impact the validity of the results?

5. What is the likelihood that the difference occurred by chance?

When you study statistics, you learn about all sorts of tools that have been invented to answer these questions.

Correlations

One of the more popular statistical methods used in psychology is the correlation. In our study, we are assuming that the presence or absence of a slide show would CAUSE the grades to be different, but all we really did was examine if there is a **relationship** between the variables. While we can identify relationships (and the absence of them), determining CAUSE is quite a bit

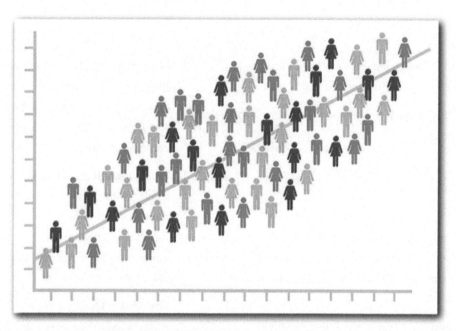

This graphic is a good representation of data that could be collected to determine a correlation. Let's say that the data along the x-axis (horizontal) is "age" and the data along the y-axis (vertical) is a measure of job satisfaction. Each person represents a data point at the intersection between their age score and their satisfaction score. The blue line that goes through the middle of the data points is called the "regression line" and it represents the average relationship between each of the data points and the mean of the group. The slope of this line (how steep and in what direction it is sloping) is the Correlation Coefficient.

One might conclude that in this sample of people, age is correlated with job satisfaction; the older you are, the more likely you are to be satisfied with your job, but does age CAUSE satisfaction?

MOVIE - Correlation and Causation

more challenging. We will need a LOT of studies to determine that and even then, it will not be 100%.

Qualitative Research

Another type of research tool are those that are qualitative in nature. As you might surmise, these methods are not bound by numerical qualities.

Qualitative research approaches research questions from a different angle. There is still a collection of data and information but the information is interpreted differently. Some of the methods and focal points of qualitative methods include:

1. **Ethnography** - the researcher immerses themselves into the culture of the individual to understand the goals, norms, expectations, and other factors associated with the situation (Example: a social psychology researcher immerses themself into a gang in a city to study how gangs work).

2. **Narrative** - the researcher examines writings like letters and diaries (Example: a personality psychologist studies the letters written between two friends to determine aspects of each person's personality).

3. **Phenomenological** - a number of methods such as interviews, watching videos, reading documents, and visiting places in order to get a feel for what happened (Example: a researcher conducting research on the Woodstock music festival).

4. **Grounded Theory** - usually follows the phenomenological approach and attempts to develop a theory as to why the event happened (Example: after studying the Woodstock music festival, theorizing about the Free Love movement and economic/political factors in play at the time).

5. **Case Study** - keeping in mind that a case study could involve a single person, a single school, a single business, or even a single country; the focus is on analyzing all aspects of that one case study (Example: a researcher in mental illness conducts an in-depth case study on one of their patients).

Both quantitative and qualitative methods are recognized as valid approaches to research. Often researchers use both methods in a single study. Let's say you wanted to do work on our original problem related to abuse. You might do a survey to determine how many individuals have successfully escaped from abusive situations (quantitative). As a follow up, you may conduct focus groups inviting the individuals who did escape to describe their experiences (qualitative).

Assessment

Chapter 2 Discussion - Ethics

Review the examples of the 20 Most Unethical Studies in Psychology. Pick one and post a comment as to why that particular study caught your eye. Then, identify which of the standards presented in the NIH Guiding Principles for Ethical Research are being violated.

In your first REPLY to a post, state how you might change the study to make it more ethical. Discuss how studies like this might have happened despite the obvious ethical questions.

Chapter 2 Quiz

1. In a single paragraph, describe why you think having a defined and disciplined research methodology is important in the field of psychology.

2. Consider the following research question: "How has the COVID-19 pandemic impacted levels of

stress in health care providers?" Identify which variable is the independent variable and which is the dependent variable.

3. Consider the following research question: "How has the COVID-19 pandemic impacted levels of stress in health care providers?" Briefly describe where you might find information about this question using an ARCHIVAL RESEARCH METHOD.

Biopsychology

3

Attention

The Gut-Brain Connection

New research is coming forth validating what we have known for a long time...the stuff going on in our gut impacts our psychology!

The Gut-Brain Connection

Learning Outcomes

Upon completion of this Chapter, students should be able to:

1. Identify the basic parts of the neuron.

2. Distinguish between different parts of the nervous system (central vs. peripheral, somatic vs. autonomic, and sympathetic vs. parasympathetic.

3. Identify and explain the basic function of the hemispheres and lobes of the brain.

Teaching

You are getting on my nerves!

Many of us have probably heard this phrase and we intuitively know what it means.

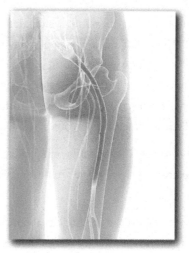

The sciatic nerve is the largest and longest nerve in the body, and sciatica (pain along the sciatic nerve) can cause weakness, numbness, tingling and pain.

Specifically, if someone is on your nerves, and the nerve happens to be the sciatic nerve, they are literally being a pain in the ____ !

Neurons and Nerves

So, now that I got that out of my system, let's talk about this! The sciatic nerve is one of many nerves in our body. Nerves, however, are kind of like ropes that are made up of neurons (instead of thread). We will begin here with a discussion about nerves, the basic building block of the entire nervous system.

The image is a simplified graphic representation of a nerve. The parts of a real nerve are never color coded like that!

1. **Soma** - this is the cell body that contains all the parts of the cell that we learn about in biology, the nucleus, the mitochondria, and other organelles.

2. **Nucleus** - like any other cell, the nucleus contains all the genetic material for the organism and dictates the life and function of the cell.

3. **Dendrites** - these branch-like fibers reach out and "connect" with surrounding cells. This "connection" allows nerves to function as a communication system in the body.

4. **Axon** - this part of the nerve cell is an elongated channel structure that communicates electrical signals from one end of the nerve to the other. The Axon is what is colored gray in what we refer to as "gray matter."

5. **Myelin** - this substance surrounds and protects the axon. Myelin develops over the lifespan and increases the efficiency and speed of neuron electrical transmissions.

6. **Schwann Cells** - these are the surrounding cells that actually produce the myelin that makes up the myelin sheath.

Neuron Anatomy

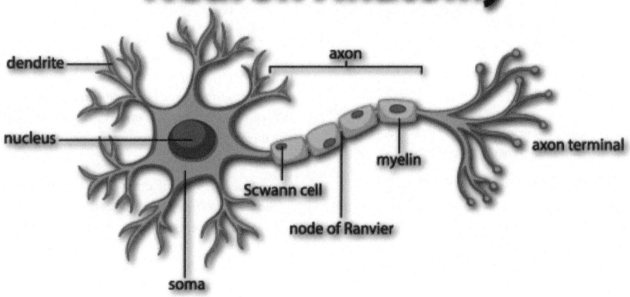

dendrite

axon

nucleus

axon terminal

Scwann cell

myelin

node of Ranvier

soma

7. **Nodes of Ranvier** - these tiny spaces in-between sections of myelin (making it look like a string of sausages) serve an important function in the speed of communication. We will discuss this function as we talk about how neurons communicate.

8. **Axon Terminal** - at the end of the axon (on many neurons) there are structures that initiate the biochemicalelectrical process we will discuss next. These terminal structures communicate with the next neuron's dendrites.

Biochemicalelectrical Communication

This part of the human body is an absolute miracle to behold! We have come to understand the process of neuron communication very well, but we are still just on the edge of understanding how this all adds up to something like appreciating a piece of music or having a nightmare.

This complicated process involves a number of components, all of which are in the name! These are cells (bio) that communicate with each other using chemicals and electrical signals.

Nerve Impulses

Throughout the structure of the neuron, electrical potential is built up through the active exchange of negative and positive chemical ions across the membrane of the cell. Specific structures in the cell membrane facilitate this process and then return sections of the cell to its original resting state.

We will see much later that some of the "psychotropic" medications prescribed to treat mental illness are meant to impact this process and thus, impact the brain.

Episode 3

THE CHEMICAL MIND

MOVIE - The Chemical Mind

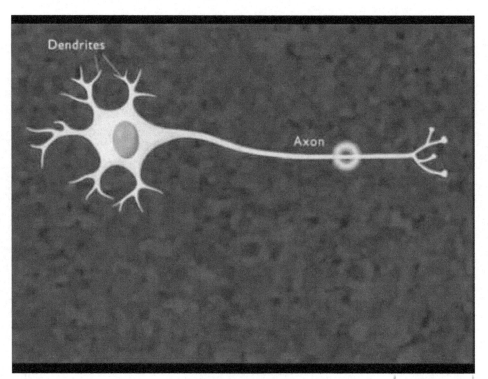

MOVIE - Nerve Impulse

Synaptic Communication

On the ends of the axon terminal are structures called "terminal buttons" which are made up of synapses. Synapses engage in a complex chemical and electrical process that allow a neuron to communicate with the next neuron.

At the synapse, changes in the cell membrane structure brought on by the electric impulse previously described release special chemicals called "neurotransmitters." The neurotransmitters flow into the synaptic gap and cross over to the adjacent cell (neurons never really touch each other, which is why I put "connect" in parentheses).

These neurotransmitters activate the adjacent cell and when enough electrical potential is built up, the process of nerve impulse starts again in the adjacent cell and the signal is communicated.

Speed of Transmission

Posted on Twitter by Bleacher Report

It is mind-boggling to consider this complex set of processes results in the lightning fast reactions of the Tom Brady and Rob Gronkowski combination (We don't real-

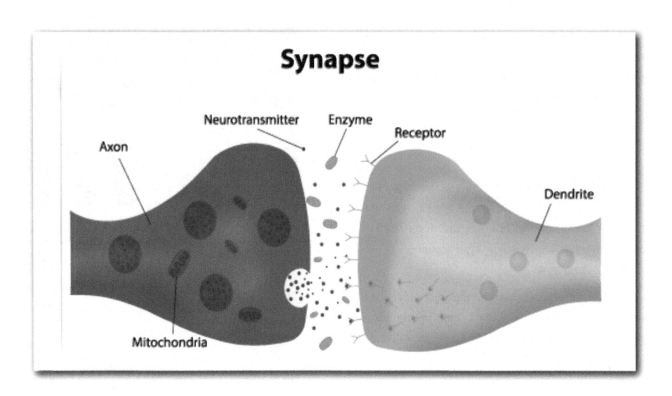

ly care because they both ABANDONED us!!!). One of the processes that speeds up the nervous system are represented in the functions of the myelin and Nodes of Ranvier.

Persons with Multiple Sclerosis (MS) have a defect in their immune system that attacks, damages, and inflames myelin. Nearly 1 million people live with MS in the U.S. and it is particularly prevalent in Maine.

Gross Anatomy of the Nervous System

Don't worry, this section is not about stuff that is "yucky!" In the title of this section, "gross" refers to larger structures. We have spent some time looking at the basic building block of the nervous system, the neuron, and the bundles of neurons we call nerves. Now we turn out attention to the larger organizations of the nervous system.

Central Nervous System (CNS) and Peripheral Nervous System (PNS)

The first division within the nervous system is made up of the central and peripheral systems. The CNS consists of the brain, brain stem, and spinal cord. By contrast, the rest of the nervous system, including all the nerves that travel around our bodies and all the different neurons are part of the PNS.

Sympathetic Nervous System and Parasympathetic Nervous System

This distinction divides the nervous system into parts that excite the body and prepare it to act under stress (sympathetic) and the part that returns the body to its resting state (parasympathetic).

When we discuss emotions we will see how the sympathetic and parasympathetic nervous systems work together to create the bodily states that we recognize as emotional states. In addition, when we look at conditions of chronic sympathetic excitation, such as stress,

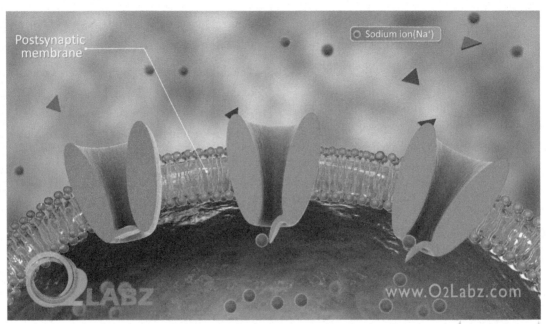

MOVIE - Nerve Synapse Animation

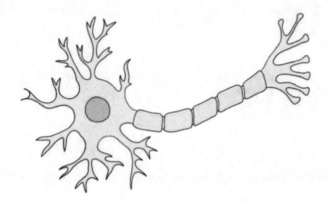

MOVIE - Myelin and the Nodes of Ranvier

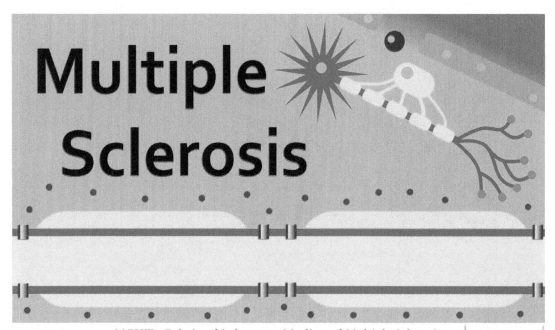

MOVIE - Relationship between Myelin and Multiple Sclerosis

chronic pain, and burnout, we can see how these organs can be impacted (racing heart, upset stomach, sweaty palms, etc.).

Somatic Nervous System and Autonomic Nervous System

The last division of the nervous system relates to how the system is controlled. You may surmise that the "autonomic" system is comprised of those aspects of our being that happen automatically. These systems include heartbeat, circulation, digestion, temperature control, and various reflexes like eye blinks and sexual function.

The somatic nervous system is the one under conscious control. These are our physical movements and, to a degree, our sensory systems.

Nociceptors - Pain Neurons

More about your experience of pain than you will ever want to know!

The following is an excerpt from Bill Bryson's "The Body":

"The experience of pain begins just beneath the skin in specialized nerve endings known as nociceptors ('Noci-' is from the Latin word meaning 'hurt.'). Nociceptors respond to three kinds of painful stimuli: thermal, chemical, and mechanical, or at least so it is universally assumed. Remarkably, scientists have not yet found the nociceptor that respond to mechanical pain. It is extraordinary surely that when you whack your thumb with a hammer or prick yourself with a needle, we don't know what actually happens beneath your outer surface.

All that can be said is that signals from all types of pain are conveyed on to the spinal cord and brain by two different types of fibers -- fast-conducting A delta fibers (they're coated in myelin, so slicker, as it were) and slower-acting C fibers. The swift A delta fibers give you the sharp ouch of a hammer blow; the slower C fibers give you the throbbing pain that follows. Nociceptors

HUMAN NERVOUS SYSTEM

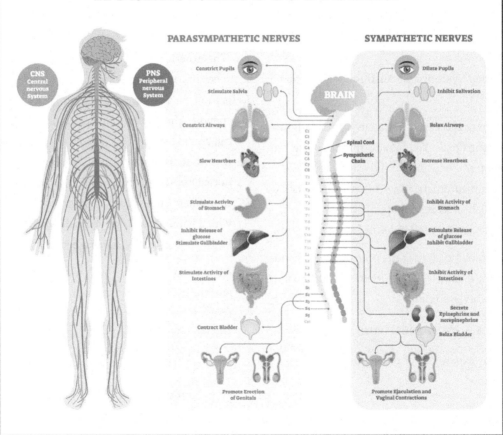

PARASYMPATHETIC NERVES

SYMPATHETIC NERVES

CNS
Central
nervous
System

PNS
Peripheral
nervous
System

BRAIN

Constrict Pupils

Stimulate Saliva

Constrict Airways

Slow Heartbeat

Stimulate Activity
of Stomach

Inhibit Release of
glucose
Stimulate Gallbladder

Stimulate Activity of
Intestines

Contract Bladder

Promote Erection
of Genitals

Dilate Pupils

Inhibit Salivation

Relax Airways

Spinal Cord

Sympathetic
Chain

Increase Heartbeat

Inhibit Activity of
Stomach

Stimulate Release
of glucose
Inhibit Gallbladder

Inhibit Activity of
Intestines

Secrete
Epinephrine and
norepinephrine

Relax Bladder

Promote Ejaculation and
Vaginal Contractions

only respond to disagreeable (or potentially disagreeable) sensations. Normal touch signals -- the feel of your feet against the ground, your hand on a doorknob, your cheek on a satin pillow -- are conveyed by different receptors on a separate set of A-beta nerves.

Nerve signals are not particularly swift. Light travels at 300 million meters per second, while nerve signals move at a decidedly more stately 120 meters a second -- about 2.5 million times slower. Still, 120 meters a second is nearly 270 miles an hour, quite fast enough over the space of a human frame to be effectively instantaneous in most circumstances. Even so, as an aid to responding quickly, we have reflexes, which means that the central nervous system can intercept a signal and act on it before passing it on to the brain.

That's why if you touch something very undesirable, your hand recoils before your brain knows what's going on. The spinal cord, in short is not just a length of impassive cabling carrying messages between the body and the brain but an active and literally decisive part of your sensory apparatus. Several of your nociceptors are polymodal, which means they are triggered by different stimuli. That's why spicy foods taste hot, for instance. They chemically activate the same nociceptors in your mouth that respond thermally to real heat. Your tongue can't tell the difference.

Even your brain is a little confused. It realizes, at a rational level, that your tongue isn't literally on fire, but it sure feels that way. What is oddest of all is that the nociceptors somehow allow you to perceive a stimulus as pleasurable if it's a vindaloo and yelp inducing if it's a hot match head, even though both activate the same nerves.

The person who first identified nociceptors -- who can indeed fairly be called patriarch of the central nervous system altogether -- was Charles Scott Sherrington (1857-1952), one of the greatest and most inexplicably forgotten British scientists of the modem era. Sherrington's life seems to have been lifted straight out of a nineteenth-century boys' adventure story. A gifted athlete, he played soccer for Ipswich Town while still in school and had a distinguished rowing career at Cambridge. He was above all a brilliant student, winning many honors while impressing all who met him with his modest manner and keen intellect.

After graduating in 1885, he studied bacteriology under the great German Robert Koch, then embarked on a dazzlingly varied and productive career in which he did seminal work on tetanus, industrial fatigue, diphtheria, cholera, bacteriology, and hematology. He proposed the law of reciprocal innervation for muscles, which states that when one muscle contracts, a companion muscle must relax-essentially explaining how muscles work. While studying the brain, he developed the concept of the synapse, coining the term 'synapse' in the process. This in turn led to the idea of proprioception -- another Sherrington coinage -- which is the body's ability to know its own orientation in space (Even with your eyes closed, you know whether you are lying down or whether your arms are outstretched and so on).

And this, in further turn, led to the discovery in 1906 of nociceptors, the nerve endings that alert you to pain. Sherrington's landmark book on the subject The Integrative Action of the Nervous System, has been compared to Newton's Principia and Harvey's De motu cordis (On the Motion of the Heart) in terms of its revolutionary importance to its field."

The Brain

"Everything we do, every thought we've ever had, is produced by the human brain. But exactly how it operates remains one of the biggest unsolved mysteries, and it seems the more we probe its secrets, the more surprises we find."

Neil deGrasse Tyson (Physicist)

The human brain remains one of the most fascinating and complex objects of study in the universe. While we understand that organ of the brain is the seat of what we call "consciousness" we are still far from understanding how all the chemical and electrical reactions of the brain add up to experience, let alone, self-awareness.

With that in mind, we can move forward and take a look at what we do know about the brain and its functions.

Basic Brain Structure

Check out these basic facts about the human brain:

1. The human brain is the largest brain of all vertebrates relative to body size.

2. It weighs about 3.3 lbs. (1.5 kilograms).

3. The average male has a brain volume of 1,274 cubic centimeters.

4. The average female brain has a volume of 1,131 cubic centimeters.

5. The brain makes up about 2 percent of a human's body weight.

6. The cerebrum makes up 85 percent of the brain's weight.

7. It contains about 86 billion nerve cells (neurons) — "gray matter."

8. It contains billions of nerve fibers (axons and dendrites) — "white matter."

9. These neurons are connected by over 100 trillion connections, or synapses.

Through innumerable studies of animal and human brains, we have a pretty good understanding of the localization of functions of the brain. For clarity, psychology has organized the brain into "lobes" and it describes the functions of our lives that are primarily carried out within each of these areas. It is good to keep in mind; however, that experience activates the entire

Episode 4

KNOW YOUR BRAIN

MOVIE - Getting to Know your Brain

Frontal Lobe

Problem solving
Judgment
Inhibition of behavior
Planning
Anticipation
Speaking (expressive language)
Emotional expression
Awareness of abilities
Self-monitoring
Motor planning
Personality
Sexual behavior
Behavior control
Limitations
Organization
Attention
Concentration
Mental flexibility
Initiation

Parietal Lobe

Sense of touch, taste and smell
Differentiation: size, shape, color
Spatial perception
Visual perception
Academic skills
Math calculations
Reading
Writing

Occipital Lobe

Visual reception area
Visual interpretation
Reading (perception and recognition)

Cerebellum

Coordination of voluntary movement
Balance and equilibrium
Some memory for reflex motor acts

Brain Stem

Sense of balance (vestibular function)
Reflexes to seeing and hearing
Autonomic nervous system
Blood vessel control
Breathing
Heart control
Digestion
Heart rate
Swallowing
Consciousness
Blood pressure
Temperature
Alertness
Ability to sleep
Sweating

Temporal Lobe

Understanding language
Organization and sequencing
Information retrieval
Musical awareness
Memory
Hearing
Learning
Feelings

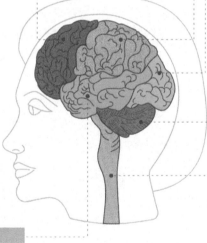

BRAIN FUNCTIONS
Segregated by Lobes

brain. There are very few aspects of our consciousness that lay simply in one part of the brain.

In the image, you can see the functions of the different parts of the brain.

1. **Frontal Lobe** - considered the location of higher thinking and executive functions such as problem-solving and critical thinking

2. **Parietal Lobe** - considered the location of sensory processing, reading, writing, and movement in our environment

3. **Occipital Lobe** - considered to be the primary area for visual processing

4. **Temporal Lobe** - considered to house the areas for processing language and hearing

5. **Cerebellum** - considered to be the center of coordinated movement, balance and equilibrium

6. **Brain Stem** - considered to house most of the autonomic processing centers

The Limbic System

The lobes of the brain tend to get a lot of attention, but it is vital to understand some of the inner structures of the brain as well. These inner structures are parts of what is known as the "mammalian brain", the part of the brain we share with all other mammals and is thought to have evolved before the cerebrum.

"The human brain is a wonderful organ. It starts to work as soon as you are born and doesn't stop until you get up to deliver a speech."

George Jessel (American Actor)

Isn't it amazing look at the list of functions that are served by the limbic system! Let's take a look at each of these and see how they are implicated in our specific experiences:

1. **Basic Ganglia** - this part of the brain is a conduit for lots of information moving around the

Limbic System

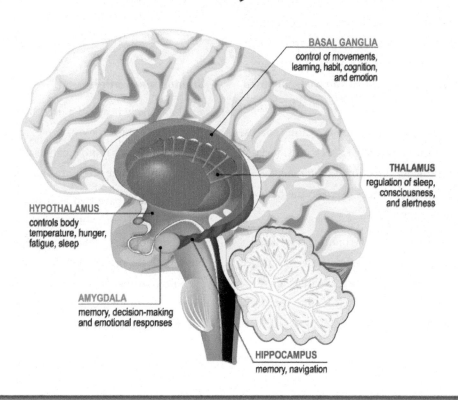

BASAL GANGLIA
control of movements, learning, habit, cognition, and emotion

THALAMUS
regulation of sleep, consciousness, and alertness

HYPOTHALAMUS
controls body temperature, hunger, fatigue, sleep

AMYGDALA
memory, decision-making and emotional responses

HIPPOCAMPUS
memory, navigation

brain. Consider that this area is deeply implicated in creating habits, good and bad!

2. **Thalamus** - this part of the brain is central to paying attention in class, your sleep cycle, and even the feeling you get when you are driving your car and go past the exit you were supposed to take!

3. **Hippocampus** - implicated in navigating spaces, women are still more likely to seek outside assistance (asking for directions) than men, despite no known differences between the male and female hippocampus!

4. **Amygdala** - this part of the brain is central to emotional responses. Paired with the executive functions of the frontal cortex, we make good emotional decisions. This may be the biological equivalent of Freud's id (we will talk about that later in the course!).

5. **Hypothalamus** - this part of the brain controls many of the "drives" we have that we will examine in the "Motivation" section of this course. This is what controls our hunger reflex and our desire for sex.

Brain Lateralization

You have likely heard of a person being "right brain" or "left brain" and you may have even heard that "right brain" people are more creative and artistic, whereas "left brain" people are more analytical and methodical.

The brain does have two hemispheres and different functions are located in each hemisphere. There is a large band of nerve fibers that connect one half of the brain with the other called the corpus callosum. However, more research is being brought to light that both sides of the brain are active regardless of the general personality of the individuals.

LEFT AND RIGHT BRAIN FUNCTIONS

LEFT - FUNCTIONS	RIGHT - FUNCTIONS
ANALYTIC THOUGHT	HOLISTIC THOUGHT
LOGICAL	INTUITION
LANGUAGE	CREATIVITY
SCIENCE AND MATH	ART AND MUSIC
TRUTH	IMAGINATION
RECOGNISE	APPRECIATE
PLANNING	PURPOSING
PLAN RUNNING	FLEXIBILITY

Right Brain/Left Brain, Right?

Left-Brain - Right-Brain Test

New Intelligence on how the Female Brain Works

How Understanding your Brain can Help you Learn

The following comes from an article summarizing the content of the book *Limitless Mind: Learn, Lead, and Live without Barriers* by Jo Boaler:

The notion that we are "talented" or "not talented" at something or another (like math or some other subject) is simply not supported by research. The brain is not a fixed entity, it is capable of magnificent change. Here are some things to keep in mind about the brain that will help you with learning.

Understand that your brain is always changing.

No one is stuck at birth. The belief in giftedness as the key to being really good at something actually gets in the way of non-gifted students' achievement.

Learn to embrace struggle, mistakes, and failure.

Practicing abilities and tasks that are actually beyond your current level is what brings about brain growth. Making mistakes actually focuses your energy on different ways to solve a problem and see it in different ways.

Change your beliefs about your mind, and your brain will follow.

By challenging your beliefs about what makes you talented (it is more about effort than it is about being "smart") your brain will respond accordingly. The old beliefs hinder your efforts and decrease your motivation to work hard.

Try multiple approaches to learning.

You have likely heard about learning styles, but these are more myth than anything else. However, experimenting with different ways to learn information can help with learning and memorizing. By studying in different ways (out loud, writing, reading, writing a song, etc.) you focus the learning across multiple areas of the brain and increase learning.

Aim for flexible thinking rather than speed.

Unless you are hoping to make a living on game shows, having the fastest answer is not really the best goal. Investing time into difficult problem solving is key to learning. Spending the time now will not only help you acquire the skills in front of you, but will make you better at learning new things in the future!

Try collaboration.

Connecting with others in and out of school to assist with your learning is a great advantage. Multiple perspectives and ideas can come about through these interactions. Indeed, one of the great educational psychologists of all time, Lev Vygotsky, specifically states that learning is "socially embedded" and happens only through the social interaction between people.

Strokes and Spinal Cord Injuries

A stroke, or a CVA (Cerebral Vascular Accident), is damage to the brain that occurs when a blood vessel bursts (hemorrhagic) or becomes blocked (ischemic). CVAs are localized so doctors often have a good idea where the damage has occurred because of the deficits in functioning that occur as a result. Damage in the occipital lobe may reveal itself with visual problems; damage in the parietal lobe may impact movement.

Spinal cord injuries, arising mostly because of motor vehicle accidents, result in crushed or severed nerves at the point of injury. Depending on how high up the spinal cord the injury occurs, the impact on the person is more severe.

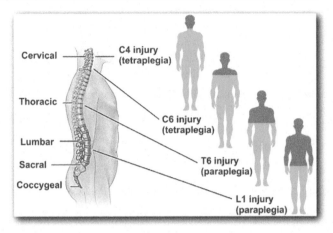

This image shows the different areas of impact depending on location of the injury. Injuries that occur above C6 are often fatal because they impact the basic autonomic function of the brain stem. However, some have survived very high level injuries and not only have restricted movement, but must have a machine help them breathe (ventilator).

This image shows Niki. In 2019 Niki suffered a C2 fracture and compression of her spinal cord. She now runs the Never Give Up foundation. Avery Biomedical Devices

Careers in Biopsychology

Does this kind of stuff really seem interesting to you? Consider a career in neuropsychology, one of the fastest growing fields in science!

The Science and Practice of Neuropsychology

Assessment

Chapter 3 Discussion - Right-Brain/ Left-Brain

Despite the relative fallacy of concepts such as "right-brain" and "left-brain," contemplating these individual differences can be fun and instructional. For this discussion, I would like you to complete the "Left-Brain - Right-Brain Test" linked in this CourseBook chapter. Report your results and provide examples from your life that agree or disagree with your results.

In your reply posts, identify individuals with similar and dissimilar traits with you. For those with similar traits, describe to them what drives you crazy about people who are not like you. For those who are not like you, tell them why they might drive you crazy (these instances would be based on the examples that the poster has included in their initial post). Also, this is supposed to be fun, so do this in fun!

Chapter 3 Quiz

This is a rather lengthy quiz with a number of different kinds of questions. The questions have you match the labels of the neuron, identify different aspects of the nervous system, and through case studies, determine which parts of the brain may be damaged. Study this material and be aware that spelling will count.

States of Consciousness

4

Attention

Daydreaming is...a good thing?

So, there you are, in class...your mind wanders (not wonders!) and you find yourself thinking of a variety of things...the next meal, homework you have due, the vacation or car you want, etc.

While we know this is not the best way to spend your time in class, there are actual benefits to daydreaming! Taking a LITTLE (yes, little, like small, tiny, short, minuscule, hardly noticeable) break can give you a boost of energy and you can reengage in the class!

The following is copied from the website associated with the previous image:

Daydreaming helps us explore new ideas and uses: In a University of California at Santa Barbara study, students who were given an extremely boring task, meant to elicit mind-wandering, were better able to come up with ideas for unusual ways to use items. That means when we're given the opportunity to daydream, our unconscious minds can think of creative solutions to problems.

Mind-wandering promotes creativity:
Another study from UCSB indicates that there's a distinct correlation between daydreaming and increased creativity. In fact, people who are more prone with daydreaming are typically skilled in being able to creatively generate new ideas. It seems that consciously paying attention to a problem isn't the best way to solve it—daydreaming and letting the mind figure it out is.

A wandering mind usually has better working memory:
According to research from the University of Wisconsin, Milwaukee and the Max Planck Institute for Human Cognitive and Brain Science, people who have a tendency to let their mind wander often have a more active and well-equipped brain, as well as a higher degree of working memory. In their study, researchers found that participants who daydreamed during easy tasks were more likely to remember information, even when distracted, indicating a higher level of working memory. Researchers believe that the mental process of daydreaming is actually very similar to the brain's working memory system.

Daydreaming can lower blood pressure:
Researchers from the Anti-Stress Center have found that daydreaming is a form of hypnosis, and can lower stress levels as well as blood pressure. People who are experiencing anxiety and stress can spend time daydreaming to relieve stress, as well as enjoy the benefits of lowered blood pressure. Further, psychiatrists from the Menninger Clinic believe that daydreaming allows you to mentally rehearse steps, such as flying for an upcoming trip, and make you better prepared to handle the events when they happen.

Reflection helps aid development and well-being:
Research published in Perspectives on Psychological Science indicates that looking inward and reflecting

through daydreaming can help us better build memories and improve our attention spans. Time spent letting your mind wander can make the quality of your outward attention better. In fact, the research proved that students who were given time and skills necessary for reflection performed better on tests, reduced anxiety, and became more motivated.

Daydreamers are better problem solvers:
Although we once thought that our minds are at rest when we're daydreaming, research from the University of British Columbia suggests that we're actually solving problems. Through fMRI scans, researchers found that activity in the complex problem-solving areas of the brain were highly active during daydreaming episodes. People who are having trouble solving complicated problems might be well served to let go of their immediate goal, and just let their mind wander with a simple task instead.

Daydreaming, like nighttime dreaming, consolidates learning:
The same research from the University of British Columbia shows that daydreaming can actually consolidate learning. It's been widely established that sleep and nighttime dreaming is an important part of the learning and memory process, but this research shows that daydreaming plays a major part as well. Need to remember what you've just learned? Instead of cramming it in your brain, daydreaming may be a more effective approach.

You can improve your IQ with daydreaming:
Allowing your brain to "rest" through daydreaming can help to improve your IQ. When daydreaming, it seems that distant areas of the brain are better able to communicate, and improving this function with practice can aid in intelligence. This is only true, however, for "good daydreaming," as in, when the mind is exploring imagination or creativity. "Bad daydreaming," like focusing on a negative comment, does not improve IQ.

With daydreaming, you can invent the theory of relativity, or win a Nobel Prize:
Noted daydreamers include Albert Einstein and Nobel prize-winning molecular biologist Elizabeth Blackburn. It's believed that Einstein's theory of relativity was born as he was daydreaming about running to the edge of the universe. Blackburn has widely noted that daydreaming greatly contributed to her success and has seen it work for some of the most creative and successful scientists in her life as well.

You can build empathy with daydreaming:
Research published in Psychological Bulletin indicates that people who daydream are more likely to have empathy. Studying Israeli high school students, researchers observed that students with high scores on the Daydreaming Scale of the IPI demonstrated more empathy than students who scored low on the scale. Spend more time daydreaming, and you just might become a more compassionate person.

People who daydream
are more likely to have
empathy.

Daydreaming
can lower blood
pressure.

Mind-wandering
promotes creativity.

The Scientifically Proven
BENEFITS OF
DAYDREAMING

Daydreaming, like
nighttime dreaming,
consolidates learning.

$$a^2 + b^2 = c^2$$

A wandering mind
usually has a better
working memory.

SOURCES: CELL.COM | BLOGS.SMITHSONIANMAG.COM | VOICES.YAHOO.COM | PSYCHOLOGICAL BULLETIN | SCIENCEDAILY.COM

Learning Outcomes

Upon completion of this chapter, students should be able to:

1. Define consciousness.

2. Discuss personal circadian rhythms and any issues with sleep deprivation or sleep debt.

3. Discuss the theories of dreams and dream interpretation.

4. Identify the neurotransmitters affected by various categories of drugs.

Teaching

I'm Awake!

Consciousness is the sum total of our awareness of internal and external stimuli such as sensations, emotions, thoughts, memories, and external stimuli from our environment. At any given point we can be said to be in a "state of consciousness" defined by the degree to which we aware of different stimuli, both internal and external. It stands to reason that when we are "awake" we are aware of more things around us than when we are asleep (more on that later!).

At this point, I want to make the distinction between characteristics of the human experience that are **states** and those that are **traits**.

Traits

Human traits are those characteristics of us that are relatively stable over time. Aspects of ourselves such as our sex, gender identity, height, race, intelligence, and personality are seen as being pretty much the same most of the time. Over the course of a typical day your traits rarely change.

State

In psychology, when we speak of state, we are talking about transient experiences that are more fluid and changing. Emotions, drives, mood, homeostasis, and hunger all identify aspects of our lives that change, sometimes from moment to moment. Over the course of a day, your states change all the time.

Biological Rhythms

As with nearly all aspects of psychology, there is some biology involved. Biological rhythms and patterns exist within both male and female bodies. These are deeply connected to the cycles of our planet and our solar system. A set that is synched with the day/night cycle of Earth are referred to as our **circadian rhythms**. Various functions in our body (and in our consciousness) cycle approximately every 24 hours and provide a rou-

tine to many of our bodily functions (heart rate, blood pressure, blood sugar, body temperature, and of course, sleep/wake cycles are a few examples).

The next graphic depicts some aspects of how the biochemical rhythms in our bodies impact our performance. While we can practice against these factors and stay up late or build up reaction time in the early evening, we are battling with biological patterns that are hard-wired into our bodies as a part of our symbiotic relationship with the Earth.

CIRCADIAN RHYTHM

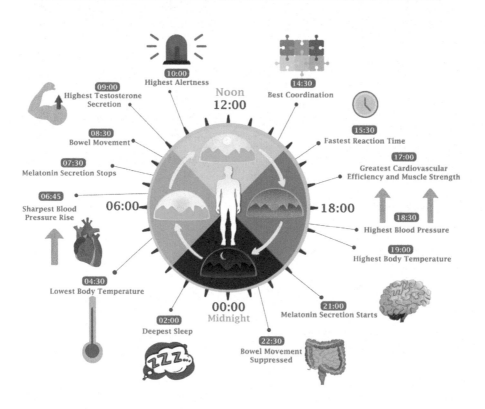

09:00 Highest Testosterone Secretion

10:00 Highest Alertness

14:30 Best Coordination

08:30 Bowel Movement

Noon 12:00

07:30 Melatonin Secretion Stops

15:30 Fastest Reaction Time

06:45 Sharpest Blood Pressure Rise

17:00 Greatest Cardiovascular Efficiency and Muscle Strength

06:00

18:00

18:30 Highest Blood Pressure

04:30 Lowest Body Temperature

19:00 Highest Body Temperature

00:00 Midnight

21:00 Melatonin Secretion Starts

02:00 Deepest Sleep

22:30 Bowel Movement Suppressed

The Brain and Consciousness

The suprachiasmatic nuclei (SCN) are a pair of structures found in the hypothalamus. Each nuclei only contains about 10,000 neurons, but they function to maintain our bodily rhythms on an approximate 24-hour schedule. Similar bundles of "timers" exist throughout the body, but the SCN is the control center.

This structure serves to regulate the rhythms of the body including the sleep-wake cycle, body temperature fluctuations, changes in blood pressure, and other patterns in our body. While the SCN can regulate these processes independent of external stimuli, it does rely on external stimuli such as sources of sunlight.

Know your Brain - Suprachiasmatic Nucleus

One of the challenges of space travel and living on other planets has to do with these circadian rhythms. In space, for example, the sun is always shining (you are not on a planet that turns away from the sun.) Astronauts on the International Space Station have to fabricate a cycle of day and night using the shutters on the windows.

As we begin to contemplate a serious effort to put people on Mars, we have to consider a few things. The National Space Biomedical Research Institute is currently studying the following Martian realities that will impact circadian rhythms:

1. Mars' gravitational pull is .38 G vs. Earth's 1 G.

2. Mars' day is 24.62 hours when Earth has a 24-hour day.

Episode 8

CONSCIOUSNESS

MOVIE - Consciousness

3. Mars' light in the sky shifts to low illumination and red, while the Earth has high illumination and shifts to blue-green wavelengths.

Each of these factors has been identified as impacting circadian rhythms and studies are underway to determine how primates will fare under these conditions.

Wakefulness vs. Sleep

Wakefulness is characterized by high levels of sensory awareness, thought, and behavior. Alternatives to normal wakefulness are referred to as **altered states of consciousness**. The most commonly known of these is, of course, sleep.

1. We spend about 1/3 of our life sleeping

2. Characterized by low levels of physical activity and reduced sensory awareness

3. Better characterized by specific brain waves

The text includes a great graphic that depicts the types of brain patters we see during specific stages of sleep: Alpha, Theta, Delta, and REM (Rapid Eye Movement).

Myths about Sleep

The following comes from a CNN report dated April 17, 2019 by Sandee LaMotte:

There is a very strong relationship between good sleep and waking success, yet there are all sorts of poor sources of information that have fueled a number of myths associated with sleeping. Here they are.

1. **Adults need five or fewer hours of sleep** - According the Center for Disease Control we should get 7-10 hours of sleep per night.

2. **It's healthy to be able to sleep anytime and anywhere** - You feel sleepy because of the presence of excess levels of adenosine in your brain (which builds up through the day.) If you don't get enough sleep you end up with excessive

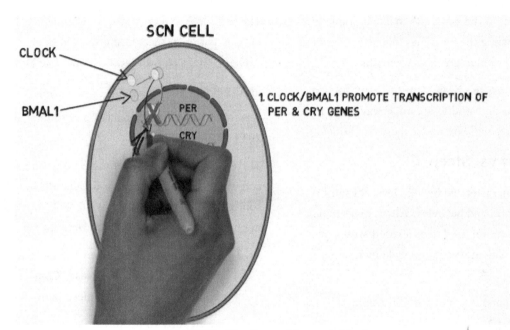

MOVIE - The Suprachiasmatic Nucleus

adenosine and a "sleep debt" that results in this ability to fall asleep anytime. This may be more of an indication of a sleep disorder.

3. **Your brain and body can adapt to less sleep -** Your body must be able to cycle through the four stages of sleep in order to benefit fully from sleep.

4. **Snoring, although annoying, is mostly harmless** - snoring is a common symptom of a very dangerous condition called sleep apnea where the sleeper stops breathing at times through the night. Not only is it dangerous, but it is exhausting because it interferes with the sleep cycle.

5. **Drinking alcohol before bed helps you fall asleep** - Although you may fall asleep faster, it actually traps you in a light level of sleep and reduces the quality of your sleep.

6. **Not sleeping? Stay in bed with your eyes closed and keep trying** - It usually takes a person about 15 minutes to fall asleep. If you are not falling asleep it is best to get up and do some mindless activity in low light (such as folding socks) until you are sleepy.

7. **It doesn't matter what time of day you sleep -** Your inner clock determines when you are going to be biochemically sleepy. Altering this schedule will result in poor quality sleep and is linked to accidents and low productivity.

8. **Watching TV in bed helps you relax -** The "blue light" that comes from your TV (and all your other devices) impacts the release of melatonin in your brain. This will result in less quality REM sleep.

9. **Hitting SNOOZE is great! No need to get up right away** - The very light sleep that you go back into after hitting the snooze button is low quality sleep.

Episode 9

SLEEP & DREAMS

MOVIE - To Sleep, Perchance to Dream

10. **Remembering your dreams is a good sign of good sleep** - Those who remember their dreams better may actually experience more brain activity than normal during the night. This might indicate that they are not getting a restful sleep.

For more information on Sleep visit the
National Sleep Foundation

Dreaming

Yes, we all have dreams. Sometimes we have difficulty remembering them. Dreaming occurs during REM sleep stages and we average 3-4 patterns of REM in a single night. Dreaming has fascinated people throughout history. In the field of psychology, dreams played a major role in the development of theories by Sigmund Freud and Carl Jung.

The function of dreams is still under debate but a number of theories have emerged:

Psychoanalytic Theory of Dreams

This theory focuses on both the manifest (actual storyline and images) and latent (conceptual and symbolic representations) of the dream. Freud felt that dreams opened the door to the unconscious and allowed our deepest desires, fears, and hopes to emerge. However, since these were emotionally powerful, the mind represented these in symbolic forms.

Carl Jung adopted Freud's interest in the latent content of dreams, but felt the symbolic representations came from a universal repository of reality called the "Collective Unconscious" rather than from the individuals' inner conflicts.

Both of these figures in psychology used dream interpretation as a major aspect of their theories and their work.

Activation-Synthesis Theory of Dreams

In this theory, the presence of dreams simply represents what the brain is so good at doing, making meaning out of meaninglessness. During REM sleep, brain activity is nearly identical to wakefulness. Given all this brain activity, the brain goes into processing the information and creating patterns even if those patterns are not there. Much the way we see shapes in the stars in the night sky.

Information Processing Theory of Dreams

This popular theory argues that the mind uses dreaming to knit together the experiences of the previous day, organizes memories, and sets to solving specific problems that were encountered. People have long reported encountering a problem and only coming up with a solution when they "slept on it."

Dream Interpretation

The practice of dream interpretation dates back to the ancient world and represents the roots of psychoanalytic theory. While interpretation in the ancient world attributed the dreams to gods and spirits, modern day interpreters rely on a mix of the Freudian and Jungian perspectives.

My personal practice of dream interpretation is one where I ask the dreamer to describe the dream in as much detail as possible. Objects, locations, activities, sensations, and feeling are all important aspects of the dream. I then consult a reliable "dream dictionary" which provides multiple interpretations of the objects, locations, and activities of dreams.

Below is a link to an Online Dream Dictionary that you can use for your own interpretations of your dreams. Remember, the purpose of this is for entertainment and self-exploration.
Dream Dictionary

Dreams and Their Interpretation

Using these as guides, I engage in a dialogue with the dreamer about what the dream may be representing in their life. It is far from being a perfect science, but it nearly always results in creative and engaging discussions...which is, in fact, the point of using dream interpretation. In the end, I will likely move away from discussing the dream and more into line with what the discussion about the dream brought up.

Substance Use Disorder

All medications and drugs have what is called a "psychoactive" effect. Indeed, as in the case of recreational and psychotropic medications, that is the point! If you read the details that come with every medication, it will describe any potential psychological impacts it may have. You may see warnings about using machinery or driving while on a specific medication, or another may cause difficulties in falling asleep. Each of these is referred to as a psychoactive effect.

Recreational Drugs and Substance Use Disorder

Drugs such as alcohol, marijuana, cocaine, and heroin are examples of drugs that are consumed specifically for their psychoactive effects. While these drugs have been around for thousands of years, their consumption has become more problematic in the modern day.

These drugs tend to imitate the naturally occurring neurotransmitters in our brain and work to activate or suppress brain activity. There are three main categories of drugs: depressants, stimulants, and hallucinogens. Drugs are characterized and organized by their overall effect on the brain. The textbook has a wonderful graphic that describes a number of drugs.

Various aspects of this concept include:

1. **Physical Dependence** - when the presence of the drug impacts the natural production of the body chemical it is imitating, and the individual becomes deficient in the chemical when not using.

2. **Psychological Dependence** - when the presence of the drug produces feelings and sensations that the individual has come to feel they cannot function without.

3. **Tolerance** - when the amount of active drug has to be increased in order for the effect to manifest.

4. **Withdrawal** - the process by which the body undergoes physiological distress in the absence of the drug.

The National Institute on Drug Abuse provides detailed information on the most commonly abused drugs.

Commonly Abused Drugs Charts

Controversial Issues

Some key discussions are being had in our society in relation to drugs and drug use. Alcohol, by far the most destructive and costly drug, is sold in grocery stores. Marijuana legalization for medical use is on the rise as is the legalization for recreational use. Finally, the opioid crisis seems to be unstoppable, with one of the only known responses to be methadone clinics which replace the opioid with another drug (a measure that is called "damage reduction").

What are your thoughts on these issues?

Mayo Clinic - Alcohol: Weighing Risks and Potential Benefits

Should Recreational Marijuana be Legal?

Methadone Treatment: The Good, Bad, and the Ugly

Other States of Consciousness

So far we have talked about three primary states of consciousness: wakefulness, sleep, and the effects of drugs. There are many other ordinary and extraordinary states of consciousness that we can attain!

Hypnosis

Hypnosis has both a therapeutic and entertainment history. It is defined as entering into an extreme state of self-focus with very little attention being paid to external stimuli. First used as entertainment to get audience members to do silly things, Freud and many other early

Episode 10

ALTERED STATES

MOVIE - Altered States

psychologists saw it as a way to get patients to relax and be more forthcoming in therapy.

Highway Hypnosis

This is a state that some people achieve when they are engaged in a monotonous task such as driving on a highway with very little variety in stimulation. We all likely have a story where we have got on the highway and driven right past our exit! In this state, we are drowsy and inattentive and we are more prone to accidents and have slower reaction times. Truckers offer the following advice:

1. Switch up your entertainment.

2. Don't neglect fresh air.

3. Be creative with a blog or vlog.

4. Smartphone use can be good (and bad).

Meditation and Prayer

Meditation is often referred to as a focusing of the mind upon a single thing (sound, object, feeling, the moment, etc.), whereas prayer is a focus on speaking and/or listening to a God. On a psychological basis, both have similar impacts. People have been known to manage their hypertension, reduce stress, and, in the case of prayer, find comfort and consolation when going through rough times.

Peak Experiences

While we will be discussing the work of Abraham Maslow when we talk about motivation, his work has relevance here. He studied individuals that he deemed as having transcended the human experience into a state he called **self-actualization**. People who are self-actualized tend to report having had a number of "peak experiences" characterized by a sense of wonder, awe, and/or ecstasy over an experience.

These may happen during life events such as the birth of a child or the vision of a sunset while camping, but the commonality is that the normal physical and psychological experience transforms into a spiritual one.

NOTE: It is not uncommon for users of opioid drugs to refer to their conscious experiences of the drug in these terms. It is no wonder that the drug is so addictive. However, these drug-induced experiences are not the same as true peak experiences and they are ultimately destructive and often fatal.

Assessment

Chapter 4 Discussion A - Sleep

Read up on the concept of circadian rhythms and the notion of sleep debt. While in school, and engaged with many other things, students often feel a degree of sleep deprivation. Discuss how this state puts you at risk and how you may address the issue.

Chapter 4 Discussion B - Dreams

History has described a lot of ways to understand dreams. Review the theories discussed in the Course-Book and the discussion on dream interpretation. Which theory do you think aligns with your thinking? Using the Dream Dictionary resource, try to interpret a dream of your own. Be open and creative in how you approach this topic.

Chapter 4 Quiz

1. Define Consciousness.

2. Select a drug discussed in the textbook that you have personal experience with (either you have used or you know someone who has used). Briefly explain the way in which that drug interacts with the nervous system, and then relate that information to the behaviors and feelings individuals may have while on the drug.

Sensation and Perception

5

Attention

Electric Taste

Our sense of taste, is one of our chemical senses. If someone ever asked you to describe what chocolate tases like, you might have some trouble. They just need to try it.

When we encounter NEW tastes, our brains attempt to find close approximations to tastes we have encountered before. As we become more adapted to these tastes, they can become unique flavors, separate from others we have experienced.

As with all the senses, there are individuals who are particularly astute at using specific senses.

MOVIE - Why do batteries taste sour?

MOVIE - Are you a Supertaster?

Learning Outcomes

Upon completion of this Chapter, students should be able to:

1. Identify the anatomical features of the eye.

2. Identify the anatomical features of the ear.

3. Provide examples of gestalt perceptual cues from the real world.

4. Discuss how other aspects of consciousness may impact sensory perception.

Teaching

Biology and the Mind

The study of sensation and perception is really a study of the interface between the biological origins of sensation from our body (from neurons specialized in picking up wavelengths, vibrations, temperature, etc.) and what our conscious mind does with this information. It can be said that our understanding of the world exists only INSIDE because we do not directly experience the things around us that are OUTSIDE.

Basic Sensation

We learned in Chapter 3 that neurons relay information around the body. There are specialized neurons that exist throughout our body that have adapted to be sensitive to specific stimuli in our environment. We have neurons in our eyes that make up the retina that are sensitive to photons of light. We have neurons in our ears that are sensitive to vibrations. We have neurons in our muscles that are sensitive to the direction we are moving, and we have neurons throughout our body that perceive temperature, pressure, and pain.

In all of these instances, however, there are basic processes taking place.

1. Sensory neurons **transduce** the external energy (light, sound, etc.) into electrical impulses that can be communicated through neurons.

2. Sensory neurons are **specialized** to respond to specific kinds of external stimuli.

3. Sensory neurons have an **upper and lower threshold** of sensitivity (there are pitches of sound so low or so high that we cannot hear them).

4. Sensory neurons have the ability to **adapt** and change the frequency of firing over time.

The Big 5

The Big 5 (my phrase) in the sensation world includes hearing, smell, touch, sight, and taste.

Absolute thresholds (the minimum amount of stimulation to activate each of these senses, for most people) are:

1. Hearing - The tic of watch from 20 feet in a quiet room (remember when watches used to tic?)

2. Smell - One drop of perfume diffused in a three-room apartment

3. Touch - A bee's wing falling on the cheek from 1 centimeter above (a moment of silence for the poor bee that donated its wings to science!)

4. Sight - A candle flame at 30 miles on a clear, dark night (wow!)

5. Taste - 1 teaspoon of sugar in 2 gallons of water

There are more that 5 Senses

While these 5 senses are well known and discussed in the textbook, we have many other senses that convey specific information to our brains. Some of these are combinations of the Big 5, but some are unique:

1. Pressure

2. Itch

3. Thermoception - Ability to sense heat and cold

4. Proprioception - Ability to tell where your body parts are in relation to other parts

5. Tension - Allow us to monitor muscle tension

6. Nociception - Our perception of pain

7. Equilibrioception - Allow us to keep our balance and perceive changes in direction

8. Stretch

9. Hunger

10. Magnetoception - Ability to detect magnetic fields

11. Time

Wow, pretty interesting isn't it!

Time for a little Physics

Electromagnetic Spectrum

As we prepare to look at our sense of vision, we want to have some understanding as to the physics of waves.

The chart describes the varied sources of energy on the electromagnetic spectrum. The defining characteristic is the wavelength, the physical distance from one peak of the wave to the next wave.

Check out this very cool chart!

ELECTROMAGNETIC SPECTRUM

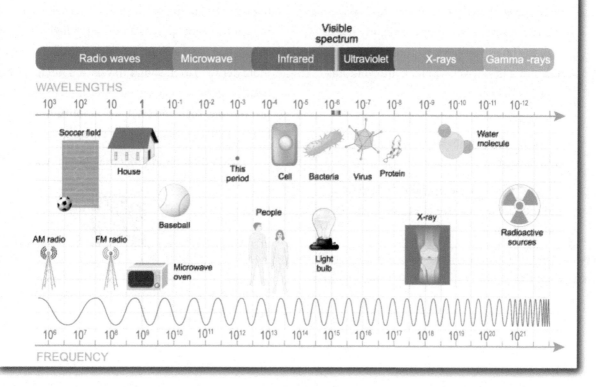

Visible spectrum

| Radio waves | Microwave | Infrared | Ultraviolet | X-rays | Gamma -rays |

WAVELENGTHS

10^3 10^2 10 1 10^{-1} 10^{-2} 10^{-3} 10^{-4} 10^{-5} 10^{-6} 10^{-7} 10^{-8} 10^{-9} 10^{-10} 10^{-11} 10^{-12}

Soccer field

House

This period

Cell

Bacteria

Virus

Protein

Water molecule

Baseball

People

X-ray

Radioactive sources

AM radio

FM radio

Microwave oven

Light bulb

10^6 10^7 10^8 10^9 10^{10} 10^{11} 10^{12} 10^{13} 10^{14} 10^{15} 10^{16} 10^{17} 10^{18} 10^{19} 10^{20} 10^{21}

FREQUENCY

1. In between AM and FM radio, the wavelength of the signals are as big as a soccer field!

2. Microwaves (like the one in your house) are big enough to see; in fact, they are slightly bigger than the holes you can look through in the door...that is why you can look into your microwave and not cook your eyes!

3. The visible spectrum, the wavelengths that our eyes can sense, is a relatively small part of the entire spectrum.

4. X-rays and gamma rays penetrate everything, and thus are destructive to our cells, our DNA, and our health.

Keep in mind that according to physics, light acts both as a wave and as an object (photon), so light is bit mysterious.

Sound Waves

Sound is transmitted by vibrating molecules through matter. Depending on the type of matter, sound transmits at different speeds. In the air (filled with air molecules), sound travels at 767 miles per hour. In water, a more dense matter, sound travels at 3355 miles per hour! Our sensation system detects changes in both **pitch** (tone, high and low) and **amplitude** (soft and loud). Different animals hear different frequencies.

MOVIE - Sound Properties (Khan Academy)

Scientists use an oscilloscope to measure sound waves, both pitch and amplitude.

Visit the Virtual Oscilloscope website with your Chrome browser!

Vision

Light is collected by the structure and specific neurons of the eyes. Specialized neurons, called **rods** (black and white) and **cones** (color) make up the **retina** layers in the eye. The information collected by all the rods and cones is sent to the optic nerve which travels to the **occipital lobe** of the brain for processing.

Review the content in your text about the eye and vision and pay particular attention to the following:

1. Iris

2. Lens

3. Fovea

4. Retina

5. Blind spot

6. Optic chiasm

Perception and Vision

Perception encompasses the processes that interpret the raw information coming from the sensory system. Perception is the brain's work when it comes to the sensation system and it creates (constructs) the world as we understand it.

The raw data that comes to our brain for processing would be difficult to recognize. It is upside down, obscured by blood vessels, blurry, etc. Our brain makes corrections to this data so we can understand what we are seeing!

These Skulls look Purple and Orange

Depth Perception and Gestalt Perceptual Cues

One of the most powerful components of human vision is our binocular vision. Our two eyes are situated on our face a few inches apart. The image received by each eye is slightly different than the other...the brain processes these images and creates the illusion of depth that we enjoy.

Some of you may remember the ViewMaster with circular cards with matching pictures. This toy worked in a very similar manner!

Gestalt psychology, an historical movement in the field of psychology, is best known for its work on perception. The **gestalt perceptual cues** are sets of rules and cues

that govern the way we see and world. In addition to binocular vision, there are other cues our eyes and brains use to determine depth. In addition, we also see patterns and we group objects together based on these principles.

Visit ViewMater today! They still exist, and now they do VR and Apps!

The Structure of the Human Eye

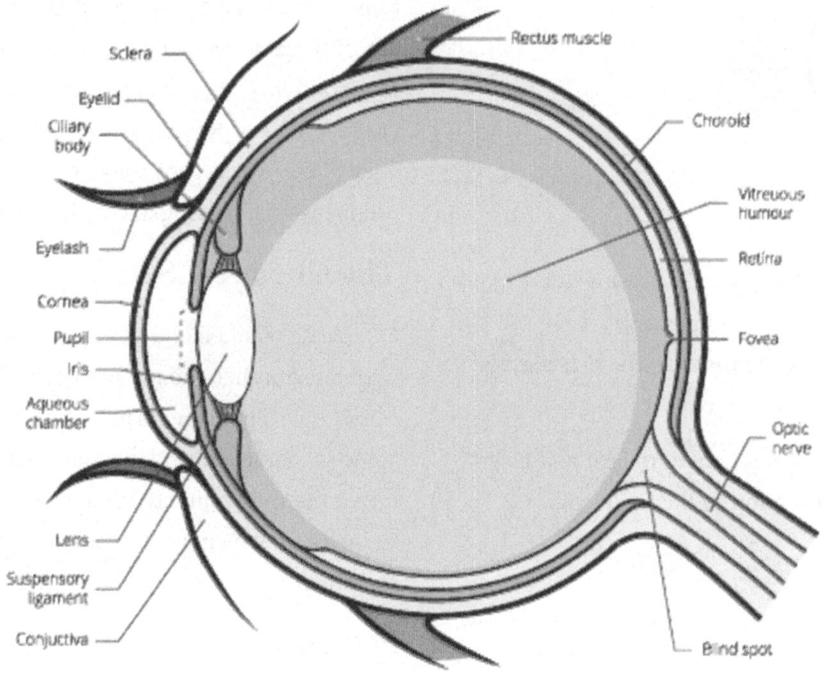

Sclera

Eyelid

Ciliary body

Eyelash

Cornea

Pupil

Iris

Aqueous chamber

Lens

Suspensory ligament

Conjuctiva

Rectus muscle

Choroid

Vitreous humour

Retina

Fovea

Optic nerve

Blind spot

Pareidolia

Hearing

Hearing represents our ability to detect sound waves within the range that humans can perceive. This includes everything from simple tones to the rich sounds of a symphony.

Review the content in your text about the ear and hearing and pay particular attention to the following:

1. Eardrum

2. Basilar membrane

3. Cochlea

4. Semicircular canals

Binaural Hearing

Similar to our two eyes providing us with the ability to see in three dimensions, our two ears allow us to localize sound in space. Small differences in the way sound enters each ear provide us with a three-dimensional view of the world. For some, this has developed into a unique way of moving about the world!

The Chemical Senses

Our sense of smell and taste are intricately connected with one another and are both considered chemical senses. We smell and taste because molecules of substance become embedded in our taste buds or our olfactory buds and stimulate these neurons to send signals to the brain which we have learned to interpret as tastes and smells.

Perception

Along with the gestalt perceptions, there are many other factors associated with how we process information coming in from our sense organs. Consider our definition of consciousness discussed in the previous chapter:

Consciousness is the sum total of our awareness of internal and external stimuli such as sensations, emotions, thoughts, memories, and external stimuli from our environment.

As our brain is receiving information from the senses, it is intermingling with all the other aspects of consciousness - emotions, thoughts, memories, expectations, etc. All of these can impact the way we experience our senses.

Your Brain Makes you think Expensive Wine is Better

Consider the following:

1. Anticipating an enjoyable activity after class impacts your perception of time. Watching the clock, it seems like it is not moving at all!

2. Specific smells can elicit very strong emotions and memories.

3. Being alone in a dark house at night may change the way you hear sounds.

MOVIE - Blind Man uses Echolocation

Animal hearing frequency range

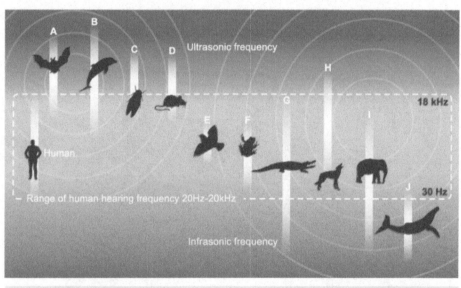

A.	Bat	2kHz - 120kHz	**F.**	Frog & Toad	50Hz - 4kHz
B.	Dolphin	75Hz - 150kHz	**G.**	Crocodile	16Hz - 18kHz
C.	Insect	10kHz - 80kHz	**H.**	Dog	64Hz - 44kHz
D.	Rat	900Hz - 79kHz	**I.**	Elephant	17Hz - 10.5kHz
E.	Bird	1kHz - 4kHz	**J.**	Blue whale	14Hz - 36Hz

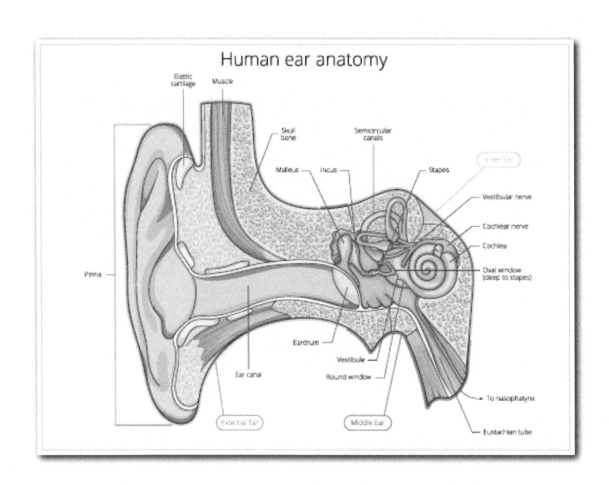

Human ear anatomy

Episode 5

SENSATION AND PERCEPTION

MOVIE - Sensation and Perception

MOVIE - The Gestalt Principles

Episode 7

PERCEIVING IS BELIEVING

MOVIE - Perceiving is Believing

HOW CAN PERCEPTION SAVE LIVES?

MOVIE - How can Perception Save Lives?

Assessment

Chapter 5 Discussion - Culture

The definition of consciousness includes the sum total of our senses, feelings, expectations, environment, context, cultural upbringing, etc. Discuss ways in which these factors shape your sensory perception.

Consider this example: Would you consider this bowl of food appetizing?

Your answer is largely based on if you were raised in a culture that views insects as food for human consumption.

Chapter 5 Quiz

1. Match the definitions to the anatomical features of the eye.

2. Match the definitions to the anatomical features of the ear.

Chapter 5 Assignment - Gestalt

Purpose

The purpose of this assignment is to develop the skill to identify examples of gestalt perceptual cues in the real world. While most examples of these gestalt principles are given as drawn images, they are all around us. Consider the image at the end of this assignment description.

Skills and Knowledge

You will demonstrate the following skills and knowledge by completing this assignment:

1. Recognize examples of gestalt principles in the real world.

2. Describe specifically how the image represents the chosen principle.

3. Upload image to the dropbox.

Task

For this assignment, you are going to use your phone, tablet, or digital camera to take a picture from your own world (you cannot search the web for images, you must find examples in your local environment).

You will take a quality picture of an example of a single (or multiple) gestalt principle(s).

You will then upload the image directly to the assignment dropbox and provide a paragraph description of the image and how it is an example of a gestalt principle in the text box of the dropbox.

Criteria for Success

Use the rubric below as a guide to this assignment.

Image   30 points

The image is an appropriate and accurate representation of a gestalt principle

Description   70 points

The description accurately describes the image and the specific gestalt principle it represents using terms from the definition of the gestalt principle

This image shows athletes at a sporting event. It is clear that you will group those who are dressed in the same color together...this is an example of the Gestalt principles of similarity and proximity.

Learning

6

Attention

The Psychology of Slot Machines

To keep players gambling, all slots rely on the same basic psychological principles discovered by B.F. Skinner in the 1960s. Skinner is famous for an experiment in which he put pigeons in a box that gave them a pellet of food when they pressed a lever. But when Skinner altered the box so that pellets came out on random presses — a system dubbed variable ratio enforcement — the pigeons pressed the lever more often. Thus was born the Skinner box, which Skinner himself likened to a slot machine.

The Skinner box works by blending tension and release — the absence of a pellet after the lever is pressed creates expectation that finds release via reward. Too little reward, and the animal becomes frustrated and stops trying; too much, and it won't push the lever as often.

Slot Machines are designed to provide users with the optimal amount of reinforcement to keep them gambling using the same principles we will talk about in this chapter, operant conditioning.

Image from Mohegan Sun Casino - Pocono Downs

bright lights, sexy images, pictures of money and winnings, haptic response (the handles shake and move to imitate old style slot machines), etc.

The Psychology of Slot Machines

However, the real "magic" is not the reinforcer, but the schedule of reinforcement. A slot machine is an example of a device that issues a VR (variable ratio) schedule of payout. No one but the owners of the Casino know when the slot is going to hit, but it has to hit often enough to keep people on the chairs putting money in. I've played music in many Casinos and the method is VERY effective.

To be fair, there are many other factors that go into the design of slot machines that increase the attraction:

Learning Outcomes

Upon completion of this chapter, students should be able to:

1. Explain how learned behaviors are different from instincts and reflexes.

2. Analyze an ad using the concepts from classical conditioning.

3. Identify and categorize real world reinforcement schedules.

Teaching

Do Humans have Instincts?

Core to the question of "nature vs. nurture," in describing the human experience, is the notion of learning. Learning can be defined as: "A relatively permanent change in behavior as a result of experience."

Most animals are born with a variety of behaviors and "knowledge" that appears to be in-born and NOT the result of experience. We refer to these patters of behavior as **instincts**. According to our textbook, instincts are "innate behaviors that are triggered by a (broad) range of events."

There is disagreement in the field of psychology as to whether humans have instincts. Keep in mind that instincts tend to produce very precise and easily identifiable patterns of behavior, such as the way a robin will build its nest. There is, however, some evidence that instincts instruct the development of certain aspects of our nervous system that predispose us to act "human"

Episode 11

HOW TO TRAIN A BRAIN

MOVIE - Crash Course Psychology - How to Train a Brain

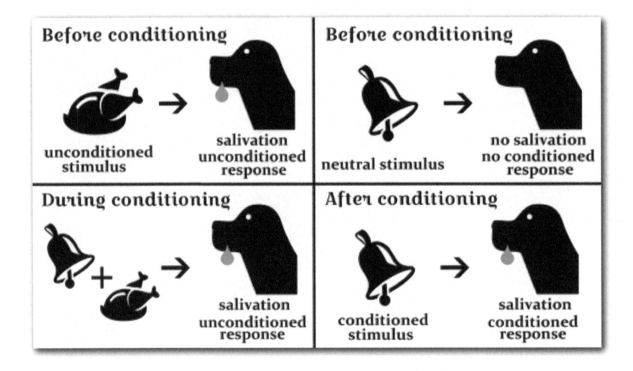

PSYCHOLOGY UNLOCKED

CLASSICAL CONDITIONING

MOVIE - Pavlov's Dog's and how People Learn

and to adapt to different circumstances. In essence, we have one verifiable instinct...the instinct to learn!

Psychology Today - How Does Instinct Work?

Drives

Another category of behaviors are those that result from biological drives. Drives is the term to describe the messages sent from the body to the brain in order to bring about a correction in our homeostasis. This means we mean that sensors in the body have picked up something that we are lacking or something that we need and it sends the message to the brain that we need to do something about it!

We have many drives such as hunger, thirst, stimulation, and sex. The behaviors themselves are not purely biological, though the root cause of them is.

Where learning comes in has to do with how we go about satisfying these drives. Depending on our cultural upbringing we eat different foods, drink different drinks, and seek different activities to stimulate ourselves. Different persons also seek different ways to satisfy their sex drives.

It is these different ways in which we satisfy drives that places them into a category by themselves and keeps them from being identified as instincts. Instincts prescribe a very specific type or pattern of behavior to satisfy the calling. This is not true with many of our drives, despite the biological origin of them.

Adaptation and Classical Conditioning

Right out of the womb (possibly even before) we begin to learn and adapt to our environment.

We start to make associations. Associations between the sounds and sights that we hear and those that meet our needs. It is a confusing and overwhelming world when we are so young, but soon we begin to associate the sound of our mother's voice with the comfort that it brings us (if we live in an attentive and loving environment!).

Classical Conditioning

Humanity has long been aware of the power of classical conditioning, but it did not get defined in the psychological literature until the pioneering work of Ivan Pavlov.

Pavlov was a physiologist who was interested in the eating and digestive aspects of animals. Having set up experiments to examine the relationship between salivation behavior in dogs and the presentation of food, he observed that dogs would often salivate when they saw the white lab coat of his assistants who prepared the food. From this point, he set up his classic experiment.

Pavlov successfully trained dogs to salivate in the presence of such innocuous stimuli as metronomes, buzzers, etc. (he, himself, never used a bell to conduct his experiments, though many illustrations of his work report that he did).

Applying Classical Conditioning to Advertising

We can look at just about any advertisement and see it in light of classical conditioning. I'll go through an example to tell you how it is done. In this process we are going to identify a few things about an ad and we will use the following "Coors Light" ad on the following pages to do it.

First, we want to know the Unconditioned Stimulus.

The Unconditioned Stimulus (US) is the part of the ad that creates a reaction, the attractive part, the part that will draw the attention of the target audience. So what draws the attention of men aged 16-80 who drink beer?

Yup, the two girls. So the twins are the US...we men did not have to LEARN to be attracted to this.

Sometimes the product is the US. This is the goal of nearly all advertisers. Good examples of products that have become US include Nike, Apple, and Coca-cola. These brand names are well know throughout the world and often need little else except the logo for recognition.

Now, we want to know the Neutral Stimulus (NS).
This is an easy one...the NS is ALWAYS the product. In this case, it is the beer.

Then, we want to know the Association.
The ad places the NS in the same place as the US...in this case, the beer (NS) appears next to the girls (US). Learning occurs when we associate these together. The association links the EMOTIONAL response of the US to the NS. So, the advertising goal is for us to think and feel the same way when we are seeing the beer as we did when we see the girls! Or at least something close to that!

NOW we have a Conditioned Stimulus (CS).
The CS is NOW the product. Now that the learning has occurred, the product itself can now be called a CS because now it brings about the same response as did the girls.

Can we know the Target Audience?
Who do you think will be attracted to this ad? All advertisements target specific people, so who do you think this ad is for? I would say that it is for all men age 16-80 who drink beer. Coors wants the target population to drink Coors beer and not Budweiser. The target audience also determines where the ad is going to be displayed. You might see this ad in Sports Illustrated but you will not see it in Quilters Quarterly Review.

Operant Conditioning

While we can say we learn a LOT through the process of classical conditioning, we also learn in other ways, such as through the process of rewards and punishments (which is, in a way, related to classical conditioning because we begin to associate specific behaviors with rewards and other behaviors with punishments).

Law of Effect

This is one of the only "laws" in psychology!

It simply states that if a behavior is followed by a positive consequence, it is more likely to happen again; if a behavior is followed by a negative consequence, then it is less likely to happen again.

The law of effect essentially defines what we mean by **reward** and **punishment**. Rewards represent anything that will make the behavior more likely to happen again, while punishments will make it LESS likely to happen again.

Keep this in mind, there is no such thing as a universal reinforcer, and not all things that some might perceive as punishments are punishments to others. A reward (reinforcement) is anything that has the EFFECT of making behavior more likely, and a punishment is anything that has the EFFECT of making a behavior less likely to happen.

A Quick Example – A

Feeling tired and groggy, tough to get focused, no motivation

MOVIE - Behavior - As Simple as ABC

The ABC Contingency Theory

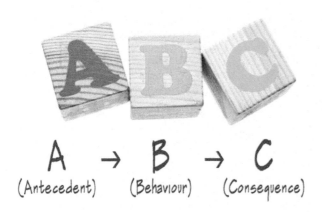

$A \rightarrow B \rightarrow C$
(Antecedent) (Behaviour) (Consequence)

The ABC contingency theory is the application of behaviorism to describe "reality." In behaviorism, the "law of effect" is seen as the primary force for explaining behaviors. The ABC theory expands on this (based on the work of BF Skinner) to include factors that occur before AND after a behavior.

A---Antecedent

Antecedents are all those environmental factors that lead up to a behavior. What is going on...what are people thinking...what signs and symbols are presented...instructions...directions...actions of others. The "A" in the ABC theory represents all the factors that may come before a behavior and may impact the course of that behavior.

Example: Instructions or directions are often the most cited "A"s in the world of behaviors. But, there is a lot to the "A"s. Instructions have to come from authority figures that we are willing to listen to...so it is much more than simply the instructions. Here is a specific example: A parent comes home and finds that the kids have been playing X-Box all day and their rooms are not clean. These observations are the "A" that may prompt behavior on the part of the parent. More on this example in a bit...

B---Behavior

Behaviors, from the point of view of this theory, are all those things that a person can do that we can observe.

It is important that we only discuss behaviors we can directly observe because that is the concern of this theory. Behaviors such as "thinking" or "believing" or even "reading" often cannot be directly observed. We can, however, create measures that would indicate that these behaviors actually did occur, even though we can't observe them directly.

That said, behaviors are actions that people can take.

Example: Continuing with our example of the parent coming home. The "A" of the observation that rooms have not been cleaned may prompt the parent to act. The "B" in this case might be that the parent approaches the kids, has them stop playing the game, and then instructs them to clean their rooms.

C---Consequence

Consequences are the effects of the behavior...positive or negative. This is where the "law of effect" is active. If the consequence of the behavior is positive, then it is likely that the behavior could occur again when needed.

If the consequence of the behavior is negative, it is less likely that the behavior will occur again.

Example: When our parent asks the kids to stop playing the X-Box and clean their room and the kids, in fact, do just that, then it is likely that in future times the parent will feel comfortable asking the kids to clean their room.

Careful observers like you might see that there are other ABCs going on at the same time. From the KIDS' point of view, they are playing X-Box and their mom comes in and tells them to clean their room (A), they decide to clean their rooms (B), and they avoid the hellish situation they have known to arise when they have disobeyed their mom! (C)

ABCs are occurring all the time all around us. It is a way to describe how the world works.

It is also a very effective way of manipulating others to change their behavior. In fact, some say it is the ONLY way to do so. The person in charge of the "A"s and the "C"s can control the "B"s!

Positive is Better than Negative

There are lots of reasons why using reinforcement is better than punishment.

1. People will work harder for the potential reinforcer than to avoid a potential punishment (consider gambling vs. speeding).

2. Delivering punishment can make the person angry and act out.

3. Delivering punishment can be an expression of anger and turn to abuse.

4. Delivering punishment teaches the person what NOT to do, but leaves a behavioral vacuum as to what TO do.

Positive and Negative Reinforcement

As I venture into this, remember that both of these are still reinforcements, therefore they both make behavior more likely.

1. Positive Reinforcement - A positive reinforcement is given to a person once they have performed the behavior.

2. Negative Reinforcement - A negative reinforcement is an unpleasant stimulus that is removed once the person has performed the behavior.

Schedules of Reinforcement

Some of the best work of BF Skinner was related to understanding how different rates of reinforcement delivery produce different patterns of behavior. This stuff is a bit wordy, but it is useful in understanding how reinforcement shapes our behavior patterns.

The textbook provides an excellent discussion of different reinforcement schedules and the pattern of behavior they bring about.

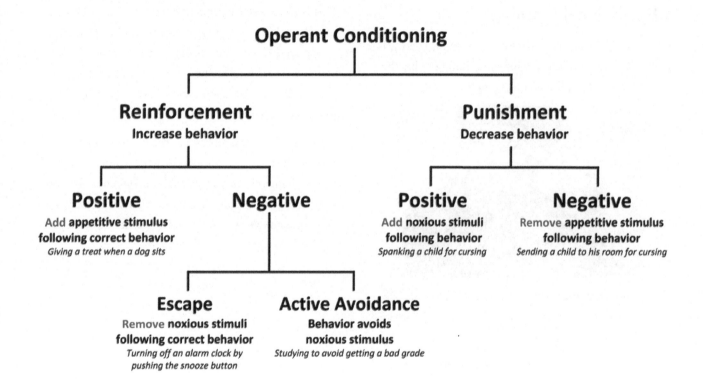

Observational Learning

Observational learning, AKA Social Learning Theory, is closely associated with operant conditioning. This theory examines the value of **role models.**

Many believe that Brie Larson's portrayal of Captain Marvel represents a much-needed female role model in the popular series of Marvel Movies and Superheroes.

People may imitate the behavior of other important people in their lives (including people they do not know, like celebrities).

This is still a behavioral model because it is not enough that the behavior is imitated, but it also needs to elicit specific responses from the environment that the individual feels are reinforcing (A teenager can act like their favorite artist, but it won't last unless it is being reinforced by others, even if it is dangerous).

Vicarious learning represents the process of changing your behavior by being in the presence of others who are receiving reinforcement and punishment. When we see others act in certain ways that elicit reinforcement and punishment, we can learn from that and act accordingly.

Assessment

Chapter 6 Discussion - Reinforcers

In many aspects of your life, your behavior is shaped and managed by reinforcers. Discuss at least two aspects of your life that involve reinforcement and describe the reinforcement schedule for each one.

Chapter 6 Quiz

1. Explain the difference between learned behaviors and instincts. In your definition, provide a clear example of each.

Chapter 6 Assignment - Advertising

Purpose

The purpose of this assignment is to apply the concepts and terms of classical conditioning to the analysis of images represented in advertising. Advertising is based upon the principles of learning by association via displaying compelling images to target audiences in close association with products. Linking products with concepts such as "beauty," "popularity," "success," and even "happiness" is key to the success of this $240,000,000,000 industry (yes, that is 240 BILLION per year, and that is only in the United States!).

By understanding the psychological factors being utilized in advertising, students may become more critical about the claims in advertising and become more informed consumers.

Skills and Knowledge

You will demonstrate the following skills and knowledge by completing this assignment:

1. Using an example advertisement, identify key components of classical conditioning as they apply to the ad.

2. Using these components, speculate on the nature of the intended audience.

3. Write a paper in a word processor.

4. Upload the paper to the appropriate assignment dropbox.

Task

Refer to the image from a magazine advertising Coca-Cola at the end of these instructions. Using this ad as an example, identify each of the key factors in classical conditioning, including:

1. Unconditioned Stimulus

2. Unconditioned Response

3. Neutral Stimulus

4. Conditioned Stimulus

5. Conditioned Response

Outline these aspects of the ad using bullet points with a detailed description of each aspect of the ad.

In a separate paragraph, speculate, based on the nature of the ad, the potential target audience of the ad. Remember, the target audience includes those who are most likely to exhibit the unconditioned response in the presence of the unconditioned stimulus. Be sure to justify your answer by outlining the relationship between characteristics of the target audience and the unconditioned stimulus/response.

Criteria for Success

Use the following rubric as a guide to this assignment:

Title Page   10 points

Standard title page with name, date, course, college name and the name of the assignment.

Unconditioned Stimulus   10 points

Correctly identified the US

Unconditioned Response   10 points

Correctly identified the UR

Neutral Stimulus   10 points

Correctly identified the NS

Conditioned Stimulus   10 points

Correctly identified the CS

Conditioned Response   10 points

Correctly identified the CR

Essay on Audience   30 points

Sound logic and rationale for audience choice

Mechanics   10 points

Spelling, syntax, and organizational structure of the paper. Clear and organized.

Thinking and Intelligence

7

Attention

What is your IQ?

Take an Online IQ Test Here!

This is a commercial site, so it will ask if you want to purchase a full profile report...you do not have to, it will send your IQ score to you directly in your email and that is all you need to complete the discussion.

From this same site you can visit pages that discuss:

1. IQ Testing and Standard Deviation

2. Test Score Comparison Chart

3. History of Intelligence Testing

Now that you have your IQ score, we will examine this score in light of other theories of intelligence.

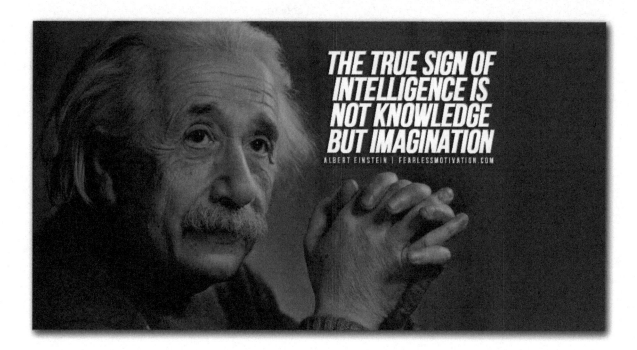

THE TRUE SIGN OF INTELLIGENCE IS NOT KNOWLEDGE BUT IMAGINATION

ALBERT EINSTEIN | FEARLESSMOTIVATION.COM

Learning Outcomes

Upon completion of this chapter, students should be able to:

1. Describe personal schemas for simple words.

2. Discuss your own experiences with the concepts of negativity bias and availability heuristics.

3. Discuss the validity and application of personal IQ results.

Teaching

What's on your Mind?

Have you ever been asked this question? Well, no matter what you answer, it all speaks to the psychological world of **cognition**. Cognition, according to our textbook, is thinking. "It accompanies the processes associated with perception, knowledge, problem solving, judgement, language, and memory."

Metacognition

For this chapter, you will be asked to engage in a process called metacognition. Simply put, this means that you are going to "think about thinking." This topic is really rooted in the philosophical foundations of psychology with attention paid to **epistemology** (how we know what we know) and **heuristics** (our habits and processes of thinking and problem solving. As in the chapter on learning, there is debate about how much of our cognitive processes are wired into the genetic composition of our brains and how much is learned. The mechanistic aspect of human cognition is the reason why the Psychology program selected the image below as the "logo!"

To orient you to the **schema** that is cognition, I'm going to list a number of **concepts** and their definitions:

1. **Concepts** are categories or groupings of words, information, ideas or memories.

2. **Prototypes** are instances that we hold in our mind that we feel best represent concepts (examples that we hold as definitions of concepts).

3. **Natural** and **artificial concepts** represent different types of concepts which can be found in everyday experience and others that are created by people.

4. **Schemas** represent clusters of concepts. If someone asked me to describe what "apple" means, the totality of my schema for apple would represent concepts of apple such as:

   - A type of fruit

   - A type of computer

   - New York City as the "Big Apple"

   - My local convenience store called "Big Apple"

   - A term of endearment, "You are the apple of my eye"

- I'm a man, so I have an "Adams Apple"

- Apple relates to Newton's discovery of the law of gravity

- An apple plays a relatively important role in the Bible's Genesis story

5. **Event schemas** (also known as **cognitive scripts**) are sets of behavior associated with specific situations that appear automatic.

Errors in Thinking

In this section, we are going to explore typical errors in judgement. There are three major errors. The fundamental attribution error will be discussed in the Social Psychology chapter. The other two we will deal with here.

As we move into these areas of human behavior, it might be important to contextualize it with a real-world example. As I write this, it is the Summer of 2020, and the world is in the middle of the COVID-19 pandemic. At the same time, the murder of George Floyd by a white police officer has sparked worldwide outrage and demonstration, with its often accompanying violence and destruction. The issue of climate change has not gone away either.

Our emotional response to these situations and the manner in which they are presented to us will be discussed in Chapter 10. Here we will address the cognitive impact of these factors and introduce the concepts of negativity bias and availability heuristics.

Negativity Bias

While we all might be desperate for some good news, the fact is, that negative things have a greater impact on our psychological state and processing than neutral or positive things. This is easy to see. We get "worked up" about negative things. How many times have you seen someone going down the road yelling at the drivers of other cars telling them how good they are driving? Even more compelling, the news reports on the rioting and looting at a few demonstrations but fails to cover the thousands of other demonstrations where none of this behavior has occurred.

Think about it:

"One thousand demonstrators are here making their voice heard - singing songs, and praying together for social change. No looting, no violence - just a clear message for change. This is Stan, live from Boston...back to you, Rebecca."

This is the news broadcast you have never heard; and, it would likely not glue you to the TV.

The network news agencies know this, and since their goal is an audience, it makes much more sense to give their viewers what will keep them in front of the TV and, incidentally, expose them to more ads. I believe there is very little actual "fake news" but the news that is there is highly selective.

The Psychological Effects of TV News

As stated in this article, this bias tends to focus the attention of individuals on negative events and news. People who were exposed to negative news were more likely to feel sadder and more anxious. Interestingly, these same individuals also tended to "catastrophize"

(making things worse than they really are) their own challenges in life! You may have even heard yourself say it right after the nightly news: "The world is going to hell in a hand-basket!" At least that is what my mom used to say.

Availability Heuristic

So why do we think the world is doing so badly when, in fact, it is not! Hold on...watch the movie!

MOVIE - Is the World getting Better or Worse? A Look at the Numbers

The term "heuristics" is the method by which we problem-solve or analyze a situation. **Availability heuristics** is when we use the information that is made most available to us to engage in decision making about our opinions and about the world around us.

If the news is constantly bombarding us with negative news and images, we can do little but draw conclusions that this is happening "all the time" or that "nothing has changed." Essentially, if I, as a white male, watch a news program on black male violence and then go out in my neighborhood, how might this effect they way I feel about that encounter?

If we only use our readily available source of data, we are, of course, going to draw the conclusion that the world is "going to hell in a hand-basket!" This perspective that we are on the verge of economic, social collapse, Armageddon, or cable cancelation is advantageous to those in power who may want to manipulate the situation to their benefit.

I'm not supporting that these dangers are not real, but they have to be kept in line with real data rather than the readily available news. To do this, we have to be

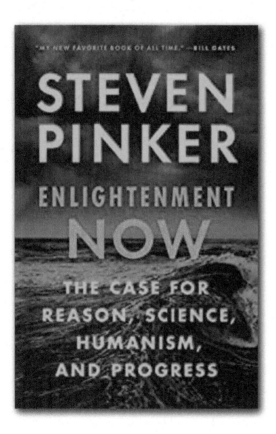

Given the 24-hour news cycle to which we have grown accustomed, it's difficult to navigate life and think that everything is peachy. But Steven Pinker has set out, first in *The Better Angels of Our Nature*, and now in *Enlightenment Now*, to illustrate that there has never been a better time to be a human being. In his new book,

Pinker points out that the slow creep of progress is not as newsworthy as, say, an earthquake or an explosion. So it's clear why we don't always have the sense that things are getting better. But the Enlightenment—with its dedication to science, reason, humanism, and progress—has led people to live longer, healthier, freer, and happier lives. And Pinker uses charts, data, history, and a firm dedication to his cause to empirically prove that we are living in better times.

It makes sense to be skeptical of a scientist arguing that that science is the answer. And his optimism won't always jibe with your personal experience or judgement.

But there's lots to chew on here—and it's so easy to obsess on the intrusions and negatives of technology and "advancement" that this book can serve as a kind of antidote.

ready to engage in our own, open-ended, non-biased research on what is true, which is not easy and not readily available.

Language

The aspect of the human experience that most separates us from the other animals is Language. No other species has such a complex set of visual, written, and auditory symbols that represent infinite possible meanings like human language. It is the highest order of expression for our cognitive abilities and accomplishments.

Language and Thought

The previously linked article is a brief, but excellent, article about the interaction between language and thought from the point of view of the Linguistic Society of America.

The relationship between language and cognition, however, is reciprocal. What this means is that as much as language is an expression of our cognition, our ways of thinking and knowing are shaped by the language (and culture) that we use.

Intelligence

A discussion of intelligence involves the psychology of individual differences as well as testing and measurement!

Individual Differences

The history of psychology has a long tradition of the study of how people are unique from one another. This fascinated early psychologists because the animal world seems so uniform among species. Individual abilities testing measured things like reaction times, specific skills, memory, etc. The tests became such a popular part of fairs and festivals that it captured the attention of the general public.

Another institution interested in individual abilities was education. In the early 1900s the French government approached Alfred Binet and asked him to develop a test to determine which students would likely struggle in public school. The test focused on measuring children's abilities such as attention, problem solving, and memory - skills they would need in school. Lewis Terman brought the test to America and it still exists as the Stanford-Binet Intelligence Test.

This was the beginning of the search to create a test for intelligence, but we have to keep in mind that the test was specifically designed to determine how well the person would do in school. Today's world has a grandiose view of a score that reveals very little.

Testing and Measurement

The subfield of psychology that focuses on testing and measurement of human abilities is called **psychometrics**. A discussion of all the details of test creation is beyond this course, but let it be said that there is a lot of attention paid to specific attributes of tests in order for them to be used professionally:

1. **Validity** - does the test measure the actual construct that it says it measures?

2. **Reliability** - does the test accurately measure the construct each time it is administered?

3. **Bias** - do aspects of the test favor one group or another in terms of the results of the test? (Bias can be present in language, structure, cultural norms, race, ethnicity, gender, and age)

4. **Test construction and administration** - is the test constructed a way that allows for accurate administration? The questions are not leading

toward specific answers? The subjects are in an environment that allows for accurate administration? Etc.

Measures of Intelligence

What follows are some examples of the different theories of intelligence that have been developed.

IQ (Intelligence Quotient)

The IQ is the first test-based definition of intelligence and it is the foundation for Binet's work. Here is an example of how it works:

1. A standardized test (see your book) is given to a child at age 9.

2. The child scores a 57 on the test (the actual score is not really relevant).

   1. We know from the standardization that the average 9-year-old scores a 46 on the test.

2. We also know from the standardization that the average 10-year-old scores a 57 on the test.

3. We conclude that this 9-year-old scored like an average 10-year-old.

4. We can now calculate the ratio between "mental age" (10) and "chronological age" (9).

$$\frac{mental\ age}{chronological\ age} = \frac{10}{9} \times 100 = 111$$

Sternberg's Triarchic Theory of Intelligence

Dr. Robert Sternberg

Moving away from the concept of intelligence being ONE THING, Robert Sternberg identified that there are three kinds of intelligence tied to the ways in which we apply them:

1. **Analytical (componential) intelligence** - academic problems and calculations, much like those measured in a traditional intelligence test

2. **Creative (experiential) intelligence** - the ability to adapt to new situations and create new solutions

3. **Practical (contextual) intelligence** - the ability to demonstrate common sense and/or street smarts (culturally situated - meaning, this one depends on the environment in which someone is asked to demonstrate common sense)

The triarchic theory of intelligence is not just a descriptive theory, but a prescriptive one as well. Here are some practical applications of the theory.

Howard Gardner's Theory of Multiple Intelligence

The other strong advocate of the multiple intelligence perspective is Howard Gardner.

Dr. Howard Gardner

It is tempting to make a couple of mistakes when dealing with Gardner's theory (or with Sternberg's theory). In applications to education, we might liken this to the notion that certain people are good at certain kinds of things and that teaching should be geared toward the types of intelligences they are good at.

This might make sense in some ways, but I doubt anyone really wants to go to school to learn things (and in ways) that they are already good at!

Truthfully, the application of multiple intelligence theory is to provide a more broad perspective of the intelligences that people have that makes life more interesting. We can then focus our efforts on developing the skills we lack.

Gardner has developed a model that identifies nine types of intelligence. Each of us has a degree of intelligence in each of them, but certain types predominate in each of us.

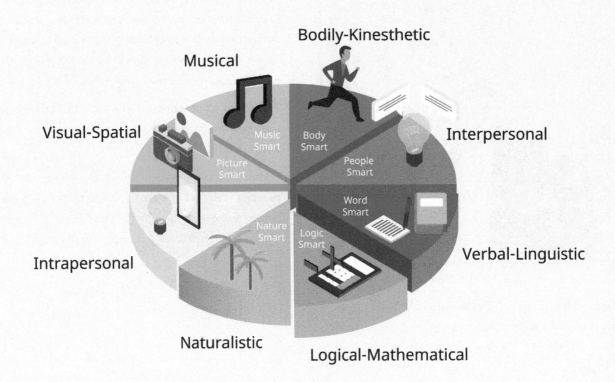

Below are links to a series of videos that Dr. Kavanaugh did on the topic of Intelligence.

Part I - G and Individual Differences

Part II - Idiots, Imbeciles, and Morons

Part III - IQ and its Applications

Part IV - Intelligence and Culture

Part V - Psychometrics

Part VI - Triarchic Theory

Part VII - Multiple Intelligence

Creativity

Creativity is the ability to generate, create, or discover new ideas, solutions, and possibilities. Habits of mind tend to characterize individuals and tasks into two general categories:

1. **Convergent thinking** - this type of practice focuses on gathering information in order to come up with a single answer to a problem.

2. **Divergent thinking** - this type of practice involves the possibility of coming up with a number of different answers to the problem.

In addition to these cognitive processes, we often experience creativity within individuals who have a lot of knowledge and experience. These two aspects of the development of schemas create **experts** in their respective field, and from those experts, we get creative ideas.

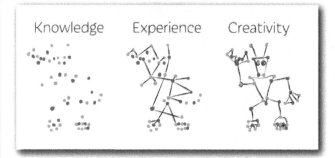

This does not mean that individuals with little knowledge and/or experience cannot be creative, but it does speak to the importance of these factors in creativity.

Switching on Creativity

Allan W. Snyder, Sophie Ellwood, and Richard P. Chi.

Most people are familiar with the phenomenon of savants (once referred to as idiot savants), individuals with significant brain dysfunction who are nevertheless able to do amazing things such as play complex piano pieces without any training after hearing them once, or count the exact number of matches in a pile in a single glance, or recall what day of the week a given date fell on from hundreds of years ago. However, we may all have the capacity for these kinds of things. Researchers have uncovered that this savant ability relates to two things. First, constraints placed on the right hemisphere of the brain by the patterns of learning and perception of the left hemisphere, so that the impairment of left hemisphere liberates certain aspects of the right hemisphere. Second, compensatory development of the right hemisphere because the left hemisphere has dysfunction. Interestingly, researchers have also discovered that they can induce heightened problem solving skills in individuals with normal function by temporarily quieting neural activity in the left hemisphere:

"A number of studies suggest that savants have some form of left-hemisphere dysfunction, together with right-hemisphere facilitation. (Typically damage to one hemisphere of the brain incites compensatory activity in the other half.) This characteristic can be observed from early childhood or after an injury, stroke or dementia, damages the left hemisphere. Some of these impairments occur in a brain area of particular interest to us, the left anterior temporal lobe. …

"T. L. Brink, then at the Palo Alto School of Professional Psychology, described the case of Mr. Z, who as a nine-year-old child suffered a gunshot wound to the left temporal lobe. He lost the ability to read and write but suddenly gained extraordinary mechanical skills; for example, he discovered he could dismantle and reassemble multi-gear bicycles without instruction. Another case is Orlando Serrell, whom we have studied, who was hit on the left side of his head with a baseball when he was 10. He has exhibited savant skills in calendar calculation the ability to swiftly discern the day of the week that a given date falls on — and in literal recall of the weather every day since his accident. The abrupt emergence of autistic-like cognitive abilities in acquired savant syndrome points to the possibility that these skills are latent in us all, but beyond conscious access.

"Intriguingly, recent evidence suggests we need not wound ourselves to access this altered cognitive state. We can quiet neuronal activity in the left hemisphere for brief periods using well-accepted forms of noninvasive brain stimulation. Many studies have shown that such stimulation can temporarily either inhibit or enhance neuronal activity in targeted areas. These techniques are now being explored for numerous applications, including the treatment of depression, eating disorders and speech impairments, among many others.

"In one recent experiment [which used a weak electric current to temporarily disrupt the firing patterns of established networks of left hemisphere brain cells], we asked 60 right-handed participants to solve a series of matchstick arithmetic 'insight' problems. An erroneous arithmetic statement, spelled out in Roman numerals using matchsticks, must be corrected by moving one matchstick.

"Participants were first given 27 problems that all involved one type of solution, namely changing an 'X' to a 'V.' The goal was to prime the subjects to become fixed in one way of solving problems. Once people have learned to solve a problem, past research has shown, they often struggle to generate solutions using a different approach. As economist John Maynard Keynes put it, 'The difficulty lies not in grasping the new ideas, but rather in escaping from the old ones.'

"The participants then received five minutes of [electric current] stimulation. Next the subjects had six minutes to solve another problem. This task required a different kind of solution. As we had expected, many people were stuck. Yet 60 percent of those in the group that received stimulation according to our parameters solved the problem. Only 20 percent of those in the placebo group solved the new problem, and reversing the direction of stimulation did not have a significant effect on performance.

"We did a follow-up study to ensure that our results were not a fluke. This time we used a notoriously difficult task — the classic nine-dots problem. The goal is to connect all nine dots with four straight lines, drawn without lifting pen from paper or retracing a line. A century of research has established that in the laboratory, at most 5 percent of participants manage to crack it, and very likely fewer manage to do so. Most people fail to decipher it even with hints and plenty of time. ... None of our participants solved the problem before stimulation or in the sham condition. Yet 14 out of 33 individuals did so as a result of receiving stimulation at the anterior temporal lobes according to our protocol. We calculated that the probability that this fraction of people could solve it by chance is less than one in a billion."

Schools and Creativity

Encouraging creativity should be a primary goal of education at all levels. Check out the video below by Sir Ken Robinson regarding schools and creativity!

Do Schools Kill Creativity?

New Study on Listening to Music and Creativity

Assessment

Chapter 7 Discussion A - Bias

In this chapter, we explored negativity bias and availability heuristics. Watch the video by Steven Pinker and discuss your own personal experiences with these two concepts. How do you feel about the portrayal of the world in the media and the perspective that Pinker provides in his TED talk?

Chapter 7 Discussion B - IQ

Take the personal IQ test below.

Take the IQ Test

This is a commercial site, so it will ask if you want to purchase a full profile report...you do not have to, it will send your IQ score to you directly in your email and that is all you need to complete this discussion.

Report your results and discuss the following:

1. Do you feel that the score is valid?

2. Would you feel it was MORE valid if you had a higher score?

3. What does this TEST predict? Is it useful for ANYTHING?

Chapter 7 Quiz

1. Choose one word from the words below and describe your schema for the word using as many concepts as you can.

   Trash | Car | Ride | Road | Love | Root

Memory

Attention

Core Memories

In the Disney/Pixar film *Inside Out*, the internal life of an 11-year-old girl, Riley, is depicted through an emotional headquarters inhabited by 5 characters which depict her basic emotions: Joy, Sadness, Disgust, Anger, and Fear.

Image from pixarpost.com

The plot of the story has to do with the management of core memories and the fact that Joy wants to keep them pure and happy and not effected by Sadness. During their adventures they visit other aspects of Riley's mind including Long-Term Memory, the Memory Dump, and the Train of Thought.

There is some truth in this depiction. According to ShrinkTank.com:

At specific moments in Riley's life, she formed core memories (e.g., making her first goal in hockey) that lead to five personality "islands" (e.g., hockey island), and when these memories were lost, her personality changed. Is this how personality development works? Probably not, but it's a really cool idea, and it does stick to some good theoretical concepts.

Personality and memories are related to each other, but not quite as depicted. One way is that personality affects what we remember and how. For instance, studies show that men who rate high in extraversion (i.e., being outgoing) tend to remember more positive moments, while women who rate high in neuroticism (i.e., sensitive to stress) tend to remember more negative moments. You could also argue that each of us do, in fact, have five personality islands (of sorts), but with far less exciting names. These would be openness, conscientiousness, extraversion, agreeableness and neuroticism (makes you miss "Goofball Island", doesn't it?).

Visit the Website

Learning Outcomes

Upon completion of this chapter, students should be able to:

1. Identify the key parts of the brain that have to do with memory.

2. Discuss, with an example, the processes of assimilation and accommodation.

3. Construct a plan to apply memory and studying strategies into your own schedule.

Teaching

How do I Remember Things?

You likely realize by now that all the systems we are talking about are interrelated with one another!

Memory is deeply connected to what we have already learned about biopsychology, consciousness, sensation & perception, and thinking! So let's break down the process of how memories appear to be formed.

The Biology of Memory

The entire nervous system is involved in the processing of memories. Starting with the brain, let's examine parts of the brain that play a role:

1. Amygdala - responsible for managing fear and aggression behaviors, and is related to memory because of the association of emotions and memories

Episode 13

HOW WE MAKE MEMORIES

MOVIE - How We Make Memories

2. Hippocampus - involved in memory recall, in particular, spatial memories and normal recognition

3. Pre-frontal cortex - implicated in the use of strategies and purposeful learning and organizing information

When we were covering the nervous system and sensation, we identified that specific neurons had the ability to convert external energy into biochemicalelectrical signals that can be understood by the nervous system. This is the process of **encoding**. We encode three types of information: semantic, visual, and auditory.

To the degree that this encoding, in its raw form, reaches the brain, the information is organized and categorized in detail. We may or may not be able to recall it later depending on the other steps in the memory process.

Sensory Memory

Our neurons and nerves hold an image for a while and then discard it. That brief period of time where the information is still in the neurons is called **sensory memory**. We can experience sensory memory when we are in the dark and someone flashes a light...for a period of time we continue to see the light even though the light is gone. This results from the fact that the neurons are still sending "we see light" messages even after the light is gone!

Sensory memory does not last a long time, though (and even when we experience it as an after image, it has already left the neurons! Once the message leaves the neurons and travels to the brain, the brain starts to work on the information.

Short-Term Memory

Short-term memory, or working memory, is represented by our ability to hold information in our mind while we are thinking about it. George Miller's work gave us the

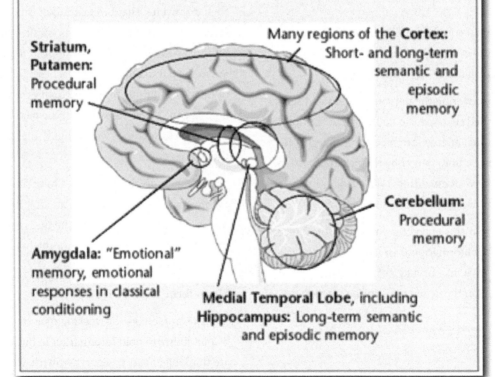

Different Structures in the Brain Handle Different Kinds of Memory

Striatum, Putamen: Procedural memory

Many regions of the **Cortex:** Short- and long-term semantic and episodic memory

Amygdala: "Emotional" memory, emotional responses in classical conditioning

Cerebellum: Procedural memory

Medial Temporal Lobe, including **Hippocampus:** Long-term semantic and episodic memory

Episode 14

REMEMBERING AND FORGETTING

MOVIE - Crash Course Psychology - Remembering and Forgetting

thought that the average person can hold 5-9 items in short-term memory at any given time (this gets translated into the axiom of 7 +/- 2).

*Dory, from Finding Nemo, suffered from
short-term memory problems!*

Short-term memory is also very volatile (meaning that external stimuli can push things out of short-term memory easily. It takes effort to keep information in short term memory.

Rehearsal

Even Paul, George, Ringo, and John had to have rehearsals!

The process by which we keep information in short-term memory for longer periods of time is called rehearsal. When we are engaged in effort to remember

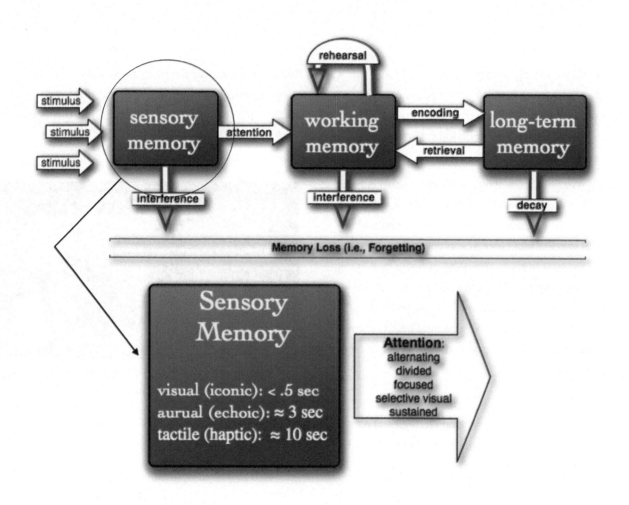

something, we usually use a number of techniques to push the information into long-term memory. We might do something over and over, say it in our head over and over, study the information many times over a week, etc.

Much of what we know about how people learn is based upon various ways in which we can engage in rehearsal so that we can remember things. I'm in a band and I engage in two distinct processes to ensure that I remember my bass parts. I "practice" at home by playing my parts over and over, and the band gets together for "rehearsal" where we all play our parts together and work on how well they blend. Note that I KNOW my part before rehearsal...and that is the difference between "practice" and "rehearsal."

Long-Term Memory

If we are successful at our rehearsal strategies, the information will be stored in long-term memory (LTM).

We are not quite sure how this is done, but certainly there are patterns of our nerve connections that correspond with specific sets of memories, but this is poorly understood.

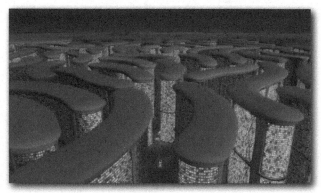

Disney/Pixar depiction of Long-Term Memory
in the film Inside Out

There are, however, different kinds of memories that we store in LTM:

1. **Explicit memories** - such as the ones that we try to remember for a test. These are memories that we purposefully try to remember.

   - **Episodic memory** - memories about specific events in our lives.

   - **Semantic memory** - memories about the objects in our worlds, such as the names of objects.

2. **Implicit memories** - these memories are formed from behaviors and are not necessarily consciously remembered.

   - **Procedural memory** - how do do physical and mental activities that seem to be automatic after we have learned them (such as riding a bike!).

   - **Emotional conditioning** - these are the associated emotional reactions we have to specific stimuli (these are largely created through classical conditioning).

Retrieval

The last part of the memory process is, of course, getting that memory out of your head so you can use it (like on a test!). The basic process of retrieval is when the brain locates the memory, it runs it through the same memory process that occurred when you learned it. So, it goes into short-term memory, then rehearsal, and then again into long-term memory.

Three factors have a tremendous impact on our ability to recall information:

1. How we learned the information to begin with, which impacts which cues will elicit the memories.

2. The circumstances that we are in when we are called upon to recall the information...the more

similar they are to the circumstances we were in when we learned the information, the better.

3. Our emotional state (including stress and motivation) will impact our ability to remember.

The Constructive Aspects of Memory

There is a school of thought in psychology called **constructivism** and it dominates much of the world of **cognitive psychology** at this time. The basic premise of constructivism is that we actively engage in our worlds in order to "construct" internal representations of our world. During this construction, we often modify both new and old information in order to bring about our own unique understanding of our world.

This process of constructing our knowledge was significantly spearheaded by Jean Piaget, who is a focus of content in your book in the chapter on Lifespan Development.

This approach to memory identifies the fact that memory is an active process (sometimes we are engaged in it, and sometimes we are not, but it is always active) and the mind is busy **assimilating** new information in our our understanding of the world, and **accommodating** existing understandings to take into account new information.

This also means that systematic and incidental errors in our memory can and do happen. These errors are outlined below in Schacter's Seven Sins of Memory:

Sin - Transience

- Type - Forgetting
- Description - Accessibility of memory decreases over time
- Example - Forget event that occurred long ago

Sin - Absentmindedness

- Type - Forgetting
- Description - Forgetting caused by lapses in attention
- Example - Forget where your phone is

Sin - Blocking

- Type - Forgetting
- Description - Accessibility of information is temporarily blocked
- Example - Tip-of-the-tongue syndrome

Sin - Misattribution

- Type - Distortion
- Description - Source of memory is confused
- Example - Recalling a dream memory as a waking memory

Sin - Suggestibility

- Type - Distortion
- Description - False memories
- Example - Results from leading questions

Sin - Bias

- Type - Distortion
- Description - Memories distorted by current belief system
- Example - Aligns memories to current belief

Sin - Persistence

- Type - Intrusion
- Description - Inability to forget undesirable memories
- Example - Traumatic events and PTSD

Problems and Solutions with Memory

As students, you are probably deeply concerned with the mechanisms of memory. While some of the material you learn in school is not vital for living or working (just interesting or a useful medium to "learn how to learn"), some of the information you are trying to learn is very important, provided you can remember it when you need it!

Memory Problems and Disorders

Much of our identity is expressed in our biographical memory (a specific part of the episodic memory that stores our life events). It is rare that we have perfect recall of any situation, but certain physical, biological, and experiential circumstances can interfere with our ability to store and/or recall life events:

1. **Amnesia** - this is the loss of memory because of an illness, physical trauma, or psychological trauma.

    - **Retrograde amnesia** - this describes the memory loss when we lose memories prior to the illness/trauma.

    - **Anterograde amnesia** - this describes when we have difficulty remembering events after the illness/trauma.

2. **Interference** - while this is implied in some forms of amnesia, we can experience difficulty due to any stimulus that interferes with the memory formation or recall processes.

    - Consider having a serious situation going on at home...this can interfere with the attention it takes to engage in the classroom, your short-term memory could be constantly filled with your situation, you could lack time to engage in adequate rehearsal, and the situation can interfere with all aspects of recall.

    - Consider other factors that may interfere:
        - Distracting loud noises
        - Illness
        - Stress
        - Being overwhelmed with information
        - Balancing work, home, and school
        - Financial troubles

Memory Solutions

One of the strongest areas of psychology is in coming up with potential solutions to memory problems, particularly the ones related to interference and the process of how to rehearse things in the first place!

1. **Life choices** - The biggest picture is recognizing that life choices such as who you are with, activ-

ities, drugs, partying, financial choices, etc. all impact how well you can learn.

2. **Trauma and events** - Managing trauma and frustrations/stress that arise in your life is key to managing learning. Getting help to deal with these strong emotions so that you can still learn can make a huge difference.

3. **Time management** - Making time in your schedule to engage in the behaviors needed to learn is vital. You cannot apply good memory strategies if you have not set adequate time aside to do them.

4. **Studying** - In college you may expect that you have already learned how to study, but this may not be the case. Different kinds of information require different strategies, and we each have our own ways of learning and organizing information. Exploring how you study (not just how much time you study) is essential to success.

5. **Memory strategies** - When challenged with remembering specific information that is, well, hard to remember, you can utilize a number of very effective strategies:

- Chunking
- Elaboration
- Over-learning
- Spaced Practice
- Mneumonics

Effective Studying

Here are some time-tested strategies for making the best use of your study time while in school:

1. Use elaborative rehearsal by "over-learning" information far more than expected and by processing information deeper (applying it to your future career, current situations, and other real-world applications).

2. Make the information meaningful to yourself.

3. Rehearse, rehearse, rehearse...engage in the same sort of recall activities you will need to do to demonstrate your memory (learning).

4. Be aware of interference. Study during quiet times and get family and friends to leave you alone!

5. Keep moving. Regular exercise is beneficial to memory.

6. Get enough sleep.

7. Study at different times of day and in different situations.

8. Memorization is best accomplished by the use of flash cards.

9. Use mnemonic devices.

Watch the following video on some excellent, evidence-based tips for studying.

THE 6 HABITS OF HIGHLY SUCCESSFUL STUDENTS

MOVIE - How to Study Effectively for School or College

Assessment

Chapter 8 Discussion - Assimilation

In this discussion I would like you to share an example of your learning where you engaged in both the processes of assimilation (of new information) and accommodation (the modification of existing information). You must provide a detailed example and use the definition of these terms to demonstrate understanding of your example.

Chapter 8 Quiz

1. Match the key parts of the brain with the type of memory function they are a part of.

Chapter 8 Assignment - Study Skills

Purpose

Psychology has long focused energy on the processes of learning and memory. Along with fields like cognitive psychology, educational psychology, and education itself, much has been learned about how people can better learn and remember information using what we know about memory.

The purpose of this assignment is to take advantage of this knowledge by identifying practical applications in your own life. We all need to remember things. While many of the things we need to remember come easily (such as our phone number and the dates of our anniversary - most of the time!), some other types of information take a bit more effort (learning content for your classes to use on a test or clinical setting).

By exploring these methods developed through scientific inquiry, you will have a wider variety of strategies for learning and memorizing information.

Skills and Knowledge

You will demonstrate the following skills and knowledge by completing this assignment:

1. Identify a variety of strategies for learning and memorization.

2. Link those strategies to specific types of learning and memorization tasks.

3. Write a plan linking specific strategies to information you will need to learn and memorize in your degree program.

4. Write a paper in a word processor.

5. Upload the paper to the appropriate assignment dropbox.

Task

Your task will be to write a paper applying specific learning and memory strategies to different tasks within your classes.

1. Review the list of strategies and the movie "How to Study Effectively for School and College" found at the end of this chapter's Teaching section.

2. Reflect on past and current learning and memorization challenges that you have encountered,

and consider the types of information you are going to have to learn and memorize within future courses in your program.

3. Describe at least three different instances where you would apply one or more of these techniques to address the learning and memorization of specific information in accordance with the following rubric.

4. Submit the written document to the appropriate dropbox.

Criteria for Success

Use the rubric below as a guide to this assignment.

Title Page   10 points

Standard title page with name, date, course, college name and the name of the assignment.

Major Plans   10 points

Write a paragraph describing your current major and academic and vocational plans.

Past Learning   10 points

Write out two instances in your PAST where you have utilized one or more of the learning and memory techniques.

Application 1   20 points

Focusing on CURRENT or anticipated FUTURE learning challenges. Describe how you plan to utilize one or more of the learning and memory techniques. Be sure to describe the type of information you are trying to learn.

Application 2   20 points

Focusing on CURRENT or anticipated FUTURE learning challenges. Describe how you plan to utilize one or more of the learning and memory techniques. Be sure to describe the type of information you are trying to learn.

Application 3   20 points

Focusing on CURRENT or anticipated FUTURE learning challenges. Describe how you plan to utilize one or more of the learning and memory techniques. Be sure to describe the type of information you are trying to learn.

Mechanics   10 points

Spelling, syntax, and organizational structure of the paper. Clear and organized.

Lifespan Development

Attention

Lifespan Development is BIGGER than Psychology!

It is likely that, as you make your way through this course, you see each chapter as a sub-field within psychology, and this is largely true. In this chapter, Lifespan Development, however, we are actually in an area of science that is much larger than psychology.

Lifespan development is said to be a **multi-disciplinary** science. This means that many fields apply themselves to understanding how people change over time. It is likely the largest field of study in the world because so many aspects of science contribute to it.

Consider the following disciplines and their individual contribution to our understanding of lifespan development:

1. **Genetics** - Understanding how our genetic code is expressed across our lifespan

2. **Medicine** - Understanding how disease impacts people at different ages and the lifespan of our immune system

3. **Biologist** - Understanding cellular-level aging

4. **Historians** - Identifying trends in aging and behavior across history

5. **Sociologists** - Examining the impact of culture and social expectations on lifespan development

6. **Psychologists** - Examining the traits of human beings and how they change (or don't change) over time

7. **Psychiatry** - Understanding how mental illness progresses over the duration of the disease and the course of a person's life

8. **Economists** - Examining human economic behavior across different ages

9. **Business** - Applying theories of lifespan development to the workplace

10. **Ecologists** - Examining human habitation such as towns and cities to determine impacts on both nature and the living environment

11. **Education** - Examining and applying learning methods across different ages through pedagogy and androgogy

Learning Outcomes

Upon completion of this chapter, students should be able to:

1. Discuss personal examples of the various clocks and forces in development.

2. Outline similarities and dissimilarities between personal age and descriptions of the historical "generations."

3. Apply Erikson's psychosocial development theory to others' stage in life.

Teaching

The Study of Lifespan Development

The study of psychology in this course has, so far, been very focused on understanding specific aspects of the human experience. These have included biopsychology, sensation, perception, learning, thinking, intelligence, and memory. The course will continue in the study of other aspects of human experience including motivation, emotion, personality, social psychology, industrial-organizational psychology, stress, lifestyle, health psychology, and finally, psychological disorders and treatment.

Each of these subject areas are presented in a way as to describe the mental processes as we understand them at this point in history. THIS chapter will focus your attention on how these aspects of our experience CHANGE over the course of our lifespan.

For example, in the subject of perception, we understand that situational factors impact the way we see things. But this impact changes over time. A rookie police officer may not notice certain cues that something criminal is going down, whereas a senior officer may see them readily. This difference occurs over time and experience on the job. Lifespan development is a multi-disciplinary study of how things change over our lifespan.

Normative Development

The utility of studying how people change is relatively easy to explain. Many careers involve working with people and assisting, in one way or another, with them changing:

1. A nurse will want to assist a person to move from an unhealthy state to a more healthy state.

2. An athletic trainer will want to assist a person to become more consistent in their exercise routine.

3. A teacher may want to teach a person a new skill.

4. A parent will want to help their children grow up to be responsible adults.

The study of lifespan development focuses on **normative development**. This means that we study how change happens in normal circumstances of aging. These would be the changes we expect as someone matures and their genetics define the patterns of their change. These are also the changes that we would expect when we live in a supportive environment and are taught what we need to know to grow up.

Many of the theories that you will be exposed to in this course, and in any lifespan development class you take, will focus on our understanding of how things change when things go as planned.

By understanding normative development, we have a better handle on how to manage abnormal experiences -

when things DON'T go as planned. We do this by applying the **developmental perspective**.

Developmental Perspective

This is best explained with an example:

You are a nurse on a medical surgical floor with nine patients. One patient is a newly diagnosed, insulin-dependent diabetic and you have been charged with teaching this person how to manage their blood sugar tests and self-administered insulin injections.

While preparing your materials, you wonder how you are going to approach this with the person, and if you are wise, you will ask a very important question: "How old is the patient?"

Why do you think this matters?

It matters because HOW you approach teaching your patient will depend on how old they are. People at different ages understand things differently, they have different motivations, they have different memory abilities, and they live in different circumstances.

By knowing how old the person is, you can customize the teaching to meet their needs.

THIS IS WHAT WE MEAN BY TAKING THE DEVELOPMENTAL PERSPECTIVE!

The theories/models of what normally happens as people change are the source of our knowledge for how people of different ages:

1. understand things differently.

2. have different motivations.

3. have different memory abilities.

4. live in different circumstances.

Forces of Change

Throughout the history of psychology, there has been an interest in the forces that cause us to change over time. One of the best ways to explain this is to use a simple analogy that everyone can understand...clocks.

Clocks mark time, they count down to a deadline, and they mark events in our lives from lunchtimes to retirement ages. The field has taken to describing the forces that cause us to change using four distinct clocks.

Biological Clock

1. The biological clock represents our natural aging process...the time when we become sexual beings, the time when are the most physically fit, the time when we start to have gray hair, and ultimately, our time to die.

2. You have likely heard this term referring to the stress that some women feel when they are approaching an age when they may not be able to have children.

3. This is also the area where the developmental question of nature vs. nurture is debated.

Psychological Clock

1. The psychological clock marks the changes in a persons cognitive and emotional maturity. It also clocks some memory development, attention span, etc.

2. When we say someone is "mature for their age," we are referring, in part, to that person's advanced state of psychological clock.

Social Clock

1. First of all...the social clock has nothing to do with being "social" like going out with friends and such...!!!

2. Social clock refers to all those standards, morals, values, and expectations about how people should behave at a specific age.

3. When people violate these expectations, we find them weird, funny, peculiar, and possibly even frightening.

4. Some of these social clocks are best characterized by the "shoulds"...

   - When SHOULD a person become sexually active?

   - When SHOULD a person have a baby?

   - When SHOULD a person move out of the house?

   - When SHOULD a person get married?

Historical Clock

1. The historical clock emphasizes all the aspects of our cultural upbringing specific to the time in history when we were born.

2. Different times in history have different expectations and primarily different social clocks

Historical Clocks and the Generations

A very popular way of characterizing the different historical clocks is by the use of the concept of generations. There is a great website (linked on the previous page) that outlines the generations from the point of view of marketing.

The following is a submission by a former student named Lisa Blue. I believe it does a good job in describing the work-related experiences of differently aged individuals. However, this description is the perspective of ONE person. There is actually a lot of diversity within each group and no one should be offended if the description does not describe them. Here is her perspective:

Historical Clocks in the Workplace by Lisa Blue

The historical clock refers to characteristics that is associated with being raised in a specific time. This is typi-

Five Generations Working Side by Side in 2020

TRADITIONALISTS	BOOMERS	GEN X	MILLENNIAL	GEN 2020
Born 1900-1945	Born 1946-1964	Born 1965-1976	Born 1977-1997	After 1997
Great Depression	Vietnam, Moon Landing	Fall of Berlin Wall	9/11 Attacks	Age 15 and Younger
World War II	Civil/Women's Rights	Gulf War	Community Service	Optimistic
Disciplined	Experimental	Independent	Immediacy	High Expectations
Workplace Loyalty	Innovators	Free Agents	Confident, Diversity	Apps
Move to the 'Burbs'	Hard Working	Internet, MTV, AIDS	Social Everything	Social Games
Vaccines	Personal Computer	Mobile Phone	Google, Facebook	Tablet Devices

Generations X, Y, Z, and the Others

cally categorized with generation names such as Baby-Boomers or Gen X.

One situation where it is very easy to see the distinctions between these generations is in the workplace.

I worked for years at the UMF Computer Center. Our director was what was considered in the Veterans group, the programmers were Baby Boomers, the networking and technicians, and myself were Generation X, and all of my student workers were Generation Y. It was very interesting to witness the different work ethics, management styles, and just ideas on life in general.

The "Great Generation"

For example, our "Veteran" director rarely checked his email, and preferred paper to digital. When he spoke, he took his time to answer a question, and responded with a "silver-tongue" as it were. He was extremely frugal when it came to the budget, and his management style was, while calm and listening, did expect solid efficient results. He worked over 80 hours a week, and rarely took any days off. Retirement was not even on his radar.

Baby Boomers

Our Baby-Boomers were very into the technology, communicated mostly with email, worked a normal 40-60 hours a week, and their management style was a little more lenient than the director. Many were looking forward to retirement, and had plans on how they were going to spend their time with travel.

Generation X

Now comes my Gen X. Technology is a huge part of our daily lives, and emails overtake the use of phone calls. Our cell phones are nearby at all times. Personally, I felt that I had a lot of opportunities and could work to accomplish anything I wanted. I certainly didn't mind starting from the bottom to work my way up in my career. I tried to think ahead towards retirement, so I saved my money as much as I could (still do). My work week was never less than 50 hours, and basically I was on call 24/7, as most IT positions are. My management style was fair, fun, focused on team work, yet not afraid to set boundaries and consequences.

Generation Y

My student workers had a very different work ethic. I would typically have to bribe several of them to show up to work on time. Constant texting and social media on the job was a constant problem. They didn't care much for authority, or feedback. And if they didn't like what we managers had to say, they could simply walk out because they could get another job in a heartbeat. Not to say that there weren't some excellent work-study students, but in general they fit the stereo-typical characteristics of the Gen Y category. They have many more options educationally and career-wise. They were raised in a society that "everyone wins", so receiving negative feedback or constructive criticism is not well-received. There is also a sort of sense of entitlement as well. On a priority scale, social time and fun ranked high, and work at the bottom.

The Historical Clock in the workplace isn't always so chronological. These days you find more Gen Xers or even Gen Y (or Nexters), in management positions over Baby Boomers. This can cause a disconnect in communication between managers and employees. Also there can be a decrease in morale in some workers whose managers are younger than the employee. Unfortunately, it probably won't be long until I'm in such a position.

Theories of Development

A full exploration of the theories that describe lifespan development is beyond the scope of this course. Your textbook describes the work of Freud, Erikson, Piaget, and Kohlberg, four very important researchers in lifespan development. For the sake of this course, we will focus on Erikson, a student of Freud.

Erik Erikson - Wikipedia

Erikson was a student of Sigmund Freud, but disagreed with Freud on a number of points...particularly on two of them:

1. Humans developed through **psychosocial** stages of development, not **psychosexual** stages.

2. Development happened across the **lifespan**, it did not end at adolescence.

Like Piaget, Erikson developed a stage theory that describes a series of tasks to be worked out between the developing psyche (mind) and society (hence the term "psychosocial" that Erikson developed).

Trust vs. Mistrust

At this stage, the child is absolutely dependent on their environment for survival. Does the environment want and provide for the child? During this first year, there is no such thing as "spoiling" a child. Responding to every cry and every laugh (as much as possible) ensures that the child will learn to trust the world and its ability to sustain him.

Autonomy vs. Shame and Doubt

We might equate this to the "terrible twos." Children are moving about in the world during the 2nd year and are getting into all kinds of mischief. They are also learning to act in the world. We need to support safe exploration and provide these opportunities.

Initiative vs. Guilt

Many parents will tell you that the "terrible twos" are nothing compared to the "terrifying threes!" At this point, the child has learned quite a bit about the world, and understands roles and expectations in the household. This is the child that may take it upon themselves to make breakfast for the family some early morning!

Industry vs. Inferiority

Note that the "school age" brings about the psychosocial conflict of "industry vs. inferiority." By this, Erikson meant that during this time, children are interacting with other children and determining, competing, and developing what they are "good at." This "comparison" and "competitive" nature of self-discovery is pervasive within the structure of schools.

Identify vs. Role Confusion

At this point, we have the opportunity to take a look at the next stage in Erikson's psychosocial theory of development. Stage 5: Identity vs. Role Confusion is really the accumulation of notions of self concept developed during the previous four stages.

Consider the platform of what has already been worked on when a child reaches Stage 5:

1. They have determined that the world is or is not a place that can be trusted and can meet their needs.

2. They have determined the degree to which they can act autonomously from others.

3. They have experimented with taking initiative.

4. They have a pretty good understanding (at least for this age) of what they are good at (when compared to others).

Upon this foundation, the child enters into the stage of identity development, which will dominate development from this point on (even though identity is specifically singled out in Stage 5, identity development is at the core of the remaining stages).

A New Stage? - Incarnation vs. Impudence

Dr. Jeffery Jensen Arnett proposed a deeper inspection of the transition between adolescence and adulthood in his 2000 article *Emerging Adulthood: A Theory of Development from Late Teens through the Twenties.*

1. Incarnation - acceptance of adult roles and responsibilities, with realistic expectations for the future and concrete plans to achieve those goals.

2. Impudence - denial of responsibility, concurrent with lack of planning, unrealistic goals, and immodesty.

Intimacy vs. Isolation

Erikson's theory now turns to the application of one's identity to the tasks of adulthood. Erikson identified that the task of early adulthood was the achievement of intimacy. We keep in mind that although the word "intimacy" is often associated with "sex," this is not the only application intended by Erikson. His notion of intimacy is inclusive of romantic relationships and sexuality, but it also incorporated deep friendships and connection to community.

Generativity vs. Stagnation

According to Erikson, the 7th stage in our lifespan has to do with achieving "generativity." Generativity encompasses procreativity, productivity, and creativity. Erikson also outlined particular "virtues" associated with each of his stages. The virtue of this stage can be said to be "take care of the persons, the products, and the ideas one has learned to care for."

Integrity vs. Despair

Here we are in Erikson's last stage of the lifespan. In this stage, people take on the task of weaving together the threads of their lives and putting them all together into a unified sense of self (integrity), and to fail to do so is to have extreme regrets and sorrows of past opportunities and decisions (despair).

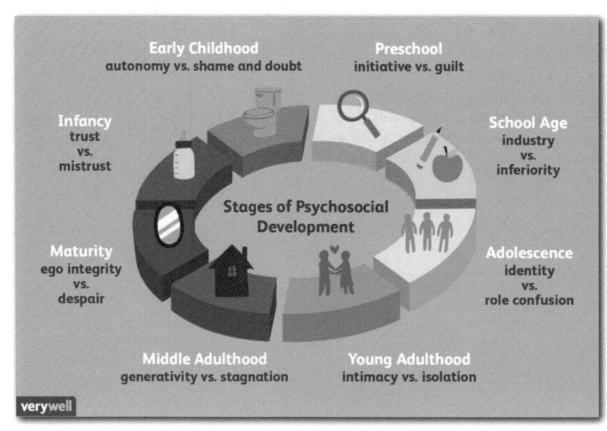

Image from verywellmind.com

Assessment

Chapter 9 Discussion A - Clocks

Review the developmental clocks that outline the various forces that shape our changes. In your main post, identify two examples from your own development that can be explained by one of these clocks. Be sure to make it clear how the example meets the definition of the clock.

Chapter 9 Discussion B - Erikson

In this discussion, I would like you to tell a story from your life that represents a significant life experience related to one of Erikson's stages that you have already completed.

In a second main post, I would like you to relate your CURRENT stage in Erikson's theory and describe how things are going.

In your reply post, select individuals in your own CURRENT stage and share the struggle!!

Chapter 9 Quiz

1. Identify your birth year and identify the generation that it aligns with.

2. Summarize the description of the generation from the following website and discuss how you do or do not meet up with this description.

http://socialmarketing.org/archives/generations-xy-z-and-the-others/

Motivation and Emotion

10

Attention

Money Does (or Does Not) Make you Happy

So...what makes you happy? What WOULD make you happy?

TED Talks are famous for revealing some of the prevailing perceptions on topics. The TED Talks playlist for "What makes you happy?" includes titles such as these:

1. The surprising science of happiness

2. Choice, happiness, and spaghetti sauce

3. Happiness and its surprises

4. Flow, the secret to happiness

5. How to buy happiness

6. The paradox of choice

7. Want to be happy? Be grateful.

8. Remember to say Thank You.

9. Less Stuff, More Happiness

10. The habits of happiness

11. The riddle of experience vs. memory

12. The hidden power of smiling

13. Happiness in body and soul

For many years the field of psychology has focused on developing a deep understanding of the dysfunctions of the human mind. Troubled minds and mental illness have dominated research in psychology for obvious reasons...people who are "well" do not need to see the "doctor"!

Dr. Martin Seligman, the Director of the University of Pennsylvania Positive Psychology Center, is leading the call to reshape the focus of psychology and include the study of "positive emotions, strength-based character, and healthy institutions."

Positive Psychology Center

Learning Outcomes

Upon completion of this chapter, students should be able to:

1. Discuss expressions of emotions in the Black Lives Matter movement.

2. Integrate measures of emotional intelligence into an analysis of self.

3. Evaluate the factors associated with your own achievement motivation.

Teaching

You've got to move it, move it...

What is the similarity between the following words: emotion, motion, commotion, demotion, promotion, and locomotion. All these words have the Latin root Movere, which means "to move."

We have all heard that a sad song or a stirring movie (there it is again!) can *move* us. Emotions are the sources of energy in our psyche. Prior to the use of the word "emotion," people felt "passions" and "sentiments." Either way, these things we know of as emotions made us *move*.

The eight basic emotions are:
Anger, disgust, sadness, surprise, fear, trust, joy, and anticipation

Plutchik's Wheel of Emotions

Robert Plutchik is a leading researcher in emotions. His theory identifies eight basic emotions (triggered by high survival situations) and a number of combinations of

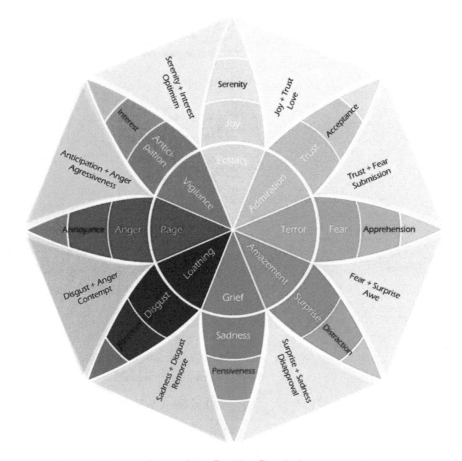

Image from Positive Psychology
There are interesting emotional activities on this site as well.

Episode 25

FEELING ALL THE FEELS

MOVIE - Feeling all the Feels

the basic emotions along with degrees of intensity of emotions to define the emotions that are represented in the following graphic.

According to Plutchik, emotions served an evolutionary-survival function. His psycho-evolutionary theory has ten postulates:

1. The concept of emotion is applicable to all evolutionary levels and applies to all animals including humans.

2. Emotions have an evolutionary history and have evolved various forms of expression in different species.

3. Emotions served an adaptive role in helping organisms deal with key survival issues posed by the environment.

4. Despite different forms of expression of emotions in different species, there are certain common elements, or prototype patterns, that can be identified.

5. There is a small number of basic, primary, or prototype emotions.

6. All other emotions are mixed or derivative states; that is, they occur as combinations, mixtures, or compounds of the primary emotions.

7. Primary emotions are hypothetical constructs or idealized states whose properties and characteristics can only be inferred from various kinds of evidence.

8. Primary emotions can be conceptualized in terms of pairs of polar opposites.

9. All emotions vary in their degree of similarity to one another.

10. Each emotion can exist in varying degrees of intensity or levels of arousal.

Theories of Emotions

So how do emotions come about? Your textbook discusses some important parts of the brain that appear to be the source and control centers for emotions. How this process actually mitigates communication between the brain, the body, and the external environment is the subject of the following theories of emotion.

Do any of these theories described on the next page seem to be more true to your experience? Can different experiences that elicit emotions be described using different theories?

Fear

One of the important emotions that we possess, even though it might be unpleasant, is fear.

Regardless of the theoretical ways in which we experience fear, the emotion itself is one that is a result of the autonomic nervous system, or the "fight or flight" response.

The term "flight or fight" refers to the evolutionary notion that when our ancestors encountered fearful situations, they either had to fight for their lives or flee and hope to get away from the danger. While this is still true in a number of frightening situations today, we experience other fears such as those in horror films or thrill rides. Clearly, with the popularity of scary films and roller coasters, it seems that fear may not always be unpleasant!

Our bodies rarely know the difference between an attacking bear and Pennywise popping onto the screen - the bodily reaction is very similar.

During this response the following changes happen:

1. Rapid heart rate (blood and energy moving in the body)

2. Blood moves away from the surface of the skin and to the muscles (getting ready to go into action)

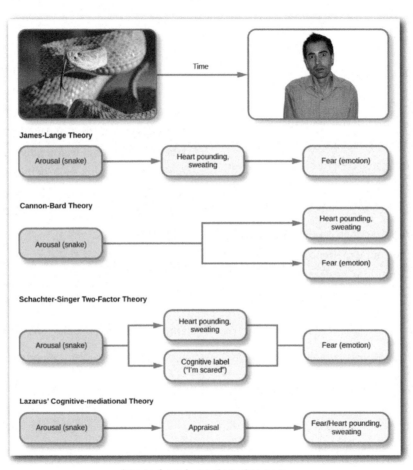

Image from lumenlearning.com

MOVIE - The Psychology of Fear

3. Dilated pupils (more specified focal area)

4. Release of endorphins into the blood stream activating the nervous system (sweaty palms and shaking)

One of the challenges of modern life is that we have social norms that limit our responses to fear (and other extreme emotions). This limited ability to respond in ways that would dissipate the added energy and chemistry of fight or flight can result in the built up of these chemicals in our blood stream. This results in issues such as chronic stress, crisis fatigue, and some aspects of PTSD.

In this video, one of the related concepts that is discussed is emotional contagion. Fear can rapidly spread across a group of people, even across a nation, because we, according to the view of evolutionary psychologists, are wired to be aware of others' emotions as they may be cues to our own survival.

Consider our ancestors. Grog comes into the cave looking and acting very scared, which triggers others' fight or flight reactions and the whole group is more likely to survive!

Anger

In my opinion, anger is one of the emotions that sort of gets ignored, yet it is so important for us to understand anger and to effectively manage it.

Anger is the combination of pain (either physical or emotional) and thoughts about the situation or causes of the pain. Various situations can bring about anger such as:

1. Things not going the way you had planned.

2. Being accused of something you did not do.

3. Being unable to find something important that you misplaced.

4. Physical injury.

These "causal" concepts are called **triggers**. Individuals can have any number of situations that can "trigger" the emotion anger. The term "trigger" really refers to a gun because of situations in which the anger presents itself suddenly and explosively.

People can also experience righteous anger. They may experience situations that are wrong and feel strongly that change needs to happen.

The ongoing demonstrations in the wake of the murder of George Floyd (and others) is an example of large numbers of people expressing anger and frustration at an unjust situation.

While some people present at the protests may have more selfish goals such as creating chaos or looting, the vast majority of participants are using their anger-related energy to force the nation to look at systemic racism and police brutality.

Both **fear** and **anger** are deeply felt by Black Americans today. Those who oppose these views also experience fear and anger. Our ability to manage our intense emotional states and engage in problem solving has become one of the most important human trails in the modern world — emotional intelligence.

Are Emotional Expressions Universal?

This comes from Mama's Last Hug by Frans de Waal.

"[Researcher Paul] Ekman set up controlled tests with people from more than twenty different nations, showing them pictures of emotional faces. All these people labeled human expressions more or less the same way, showing little variation in recognizing anger, fear, happiness, and so on. A laugh means the same all over the world. One possible alternative explanation bothered Ekman, though. What if people everywhere were affected by popular Hollywood movies and television shows? Could this account for the uniformity of reactions? He traveled to one of the farthest corners of the planet to administer his tests to a preliterate tribe in Papua New Guinea. Not only had these people never heard of John Wayne or Marilyn Monroe, they were unfamiliar with television and magazines, period. Yet they still correctly identified most of the emotional faces that Ekman held in front of them, and they themselves showed no novel, unusual expressions in one hundred thousand feet of motion pictures of their daily lives. Ekman's data so powerfully argued in favor of universality that they permanently altered our view of human emotions and their expression. Nowadays, we consider them part of human nature.

"We should realize, though, how much all these studies rely on language. We are comparing not just faces and how we judge them but also the labels we attach to them. Since every language has its own emotional vocabulary, translation remains an issue. The only way around it is direct observation of how expressions are being used. If it is true that the environment shapes facial expressions, then children who are born blind and deaf should show no expressions at all, or only strange ones, because they've never seen the faces of people around them. Yet in studies of these children, they laugh, smile, and cry in the same way and under the same circumstances as any typical child. Since their situation excludes learning from models, how could anyone doubt that emotional expressions are part of biology?"

"We have thus returned to Charles Darwin's position in his 1872 book The Expression of the Emotions in Man and Animals. Darwin stressed that facial expressions are part of our species's repertoire and pointed out similarities with monkeys and apes, suggesting that all primates have similar emotions."

Emotional Intelligence

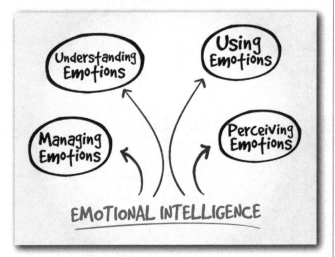

Psychologist and journalist, Daniel Goleman, is the author of "Working With Emotional Intelligence". Goleman believes that IQ is no longer as valued as it once was as being an indicator of a person's success.

Now it is emotional intelligence that has become the new yardstick. Emotional intelligence refers to areas like self-awareness, empathy, and social skills, and it is these qualities that employers are now looking for.

Take an Emotional Intelligence Test

Motivation

Motivation is another word derived from the Latin root movere. Motivation is of key concern to psychologists because many believe that most of our behaviors involve some sort of motivation. Aside from those we learned through classical and operant Conditioning, the cognitive learning that we engage in is spurned on by the motivation of the individual.

MOVIE - Emotional Intelligence

Episode 17

THE POWER OF MOTIVATION

MOVIE - The Power of Motivation

Maslow's Hierarchy of Needs

One of the most famous of the theories of motivation was put together by humanist psychologist, Abraham Maslow.

Maslow's main contention, much in opposition to the prevailing behaviorist mentality of the day in the U.S., was that each of us possesses an innate tendency toward self-actualization, or the fulfillment of our potential.

Maslow began to study the lives of persons he felt were self-actualized and concluded that they all had any number of the following traits:

1. An objective perception of reality

2. A full acceptance of their own nature

3. A commitment and dedication to some kind of work

4. Simplicity and naturalness of behavior

5. A need for autonomy, privacy, and independence

6. Intense mystical or peak experiences

7. Empathy with, and affection for, all humanity

8. Resistance to conformity

9. A democratic character structure

10. An attitude of creativeness

11. A high degree of what Adler termed "social interest"

Self-actualization
desire to become the most that one can be

Esteem
respect, self-esteem, status, recognition, strength, freedom

Love and belonging
friendship, intimacy, family, sense of connection

Safety needs
personal security, employment, resources, health, property

Physiological needs
air, water, food, shelter, sleep, clothing, reproduction

However, he postulated that we had to first satisfy lower needs in order to prepare for self-actualization. This was the beginning of his famous hierarchy of needs.

Achievement and Motivation

An interesting area of exploration in psychology, and a chief focal point for research in positive psychology, is achievement.

What factors are important in achievement? How come some people seem to be successful, while others are not? To address this area, I'm going to cover a number of notions in the following section. Consider how each of these plays a role in your own achievement process.

Learned Motives

Through the process of socialization we learned to value certain things. Our culture taught us what "accomplishment" and "success" mean, and we often take these ideas on as our own, thinking that they came from within rather than being taught.

Social Motives

Social motives are those that are focused on achieving status in your social groups. This can be through work, sports, hobbies, knowledge, degrees, etc. But they are learned to be of value in your social groups.

Need for Achievement

Many of us were taught that "doing a good job" was important. This is related to social motives, but we may refine these to suit our interests. David McClelland's theory of motivation lists need for achievement (n-ach) as a basic human need.

Power and Control

Many of us can likely relate to stories about times we felt our "lives were out of control." These are uncomfortable times and we work hard to regain control. Issues that arise when someone is dying or when they are burned out at work have much to do with control. Mc-

Clelland's theory of motivation lists need for authority and power (n-pow) as a basic human need.

Affiliation

Although there are loners out there, we are primarily a social animal. Friends, family, workgroups, school connections, etc. are important aspects of our lives and we are motivated to act so that we can achieve and sustain "membership." McClelland's third basic human need is a need for affiliation (n-affil).

Fear of Failure

Despite its connotation as a "bad thing," fear of failure is actually a necessary component of success! How hard would you really work in this class if you were already guaranteed an A? The current trend of "everyone wins" and "everyone makes the team and gets a trophy" is certainly appropriate for very young children, but not for everyone else.

Self-Handicapping

Self-handicapping is a complex cognitive process that people use to "justify" failure so as to not focus on personal attributes that contributed to the failure. In a word, these are excuses, denials of talent, lack of effort, blaming, sabotaging, and of course, the infamous procrastination.

Procrastination

The final concept I want you to contemplate is procrastination, as it is very likely something that you experience, maybe quite often. A quick explanation of this concept is as follows:

1. A person has a high n-ach and n-affil.

2. Fear of failure is present...meaning there is a real and present risk of failure.

3. The individual is faced with a task that is high cognitive load and perceives that they may or may not do well on the task.

4. The person chooses to avoid the task and does not complete it.

5. While the individual takes a n-ach hit, they are able to "save face" both with themselves and others by arguing that they would have done well if they would have done it.

Sound familiar?

Assessment

Chapter 10 Discussion - Anger

Anger, in my opinion, is the emotion that gets shunned a lot. Sadly, anger is often associated with acting out and violence. Yet, there are times in which we are justifiably angry and many people have difficulty dealing with this emotion.

Share instances of justified anger, your own or others, and discuss ways in which anger can be expressed appropriately. Consider also the feelings of anger "in the moment", what can we do with these strong emotions?

Chapter 10 Quiz

1. Take the emotional intelligence test and report your score. Provide a brief profile from your results and report on how accurate the test was in describing your emotional intelligence

2. Select one of the following concepts and a) define it, and then b) describe how this construct

has played an important role in your own learning and motivation.

1. Learned Motives

2. Social Motives

3. Achievement Motivation

4. Affiliation

5. Fear of Failure

Personality

11

Attention

The "Humors" are Alive and Well!

The idea of the four temperaments traces back to an Ancient Greek medical theory that there were four fundamental bodily humors (blood, yellow bile, black bile, and phlegm) which could cause illness if they were out of balance. The terms sanguine, choleric, melancholic and phlegmatic were coined by the Greek physician Aelius Galenus to describe the effect of these humors on human behavior. This idea is perhaps one of the oldest that looks like a theory of personality.

The four temperaments have never been a part of modern medicine or psychological science, but remain fairly well known due to their use by self-help and spirituality authors.

The Sanguine Temperament   The Choleric Temperament   The Melancholic Temperament   The Phlegmatic Temperament

Greek statuary exemplifying the Sanguine, Choleric, Melancholic, and Phlegmatic personality types as identified by the early Greeks.

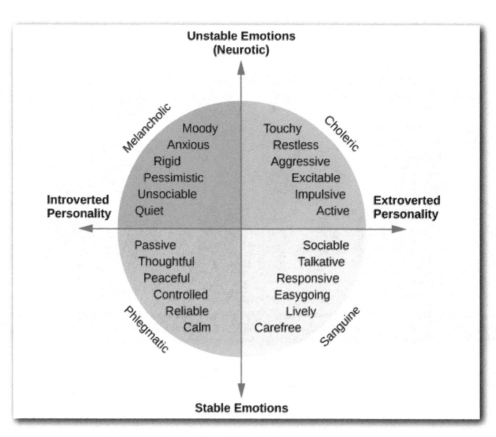

Image from lumenlearning.com

OSPP Four Temperaments Test

Learn more about this and other aspects of early Greek
medicine!

Learning Outcomes

Upon completion of this chapter, students should be able to:

1. Discuss the contributions to our understanding of personality by Sigmund Freud.

2. Apply the results of both trait and type personality test results to an understanding of self.

Teaching

Who are you?...who...who...who...who!

British rockers "The Who" asked this question on their album release of "Who are You" in 1978. Psychology has been asking this question for a LOT longer.

Theories of Personality

Similar to the study of intelligence, the study of personality is elusive and is described by a great number of theories. So, let's start with a definition of what all those theories are trying to examine.

According to our textbook, personality "refers to the long-standing traits and patterns that propel individuals to consistently think, feel, and behave in specific ways."

The key word here is "consistent." Throughout this course we have been learning about factors that contribute to our behavior but at this point ,we are looking at that aspect of ourselves that is "consistent" across most situations. These are the patterns of behavior that define who we are to ourselves and to others. While we undergo mood fluctuations rapidly at times, our personality tends to remain consistent. In fact, we focus on the parts that ARE consistent and call them "personality."

Theories of personality exist to attempt to understand the ways in which we are all different from one another and reflect different ideas about how the mind works. Your textbook does an excellent job of reviewing the early attempts of defining personality through the Greek "humors" and the pseudoscience, but once lucrative field of "phrenology."

Measuring Personality

Each of these different approaches to personality were challenged with ways to differentiate individual variations between people. Over the years, these methods were as diverse (and often unscientific) as the theories themselves. However, in the later years of the field, methods for measuring all kinds of psychological phenomena, including personality, began to emerge.

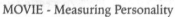

MOVIE - Measuring Personality

Sigmund Freud

There is probably no singular name better known in the field of psychology than Sigmund Freud. Born in 1856, Freud was a physiologist with an interest in the new field of psychology as he graduated with is MD in 1881. During his work at the Vienna General Hospital, he be-gan his investigations into the cause of mental illness and turned his field upside down.

While a full examination of Freud's work is beyond the scope of this course, he is credited with introducing the clinical applications of talk therapy, dream interpretation, free association, ego defense mechanisms, the conscious and unconscious mind, human developmental stages, and of course, personality. For the sake of this chapter we are going to focus on his ideas on the structure and function of the personality.

It is important to understand that Freud, a physician, was committed to trying to understand the cause of the problems his patients presented to him.

He was, first and foremost, a doctor and spent much of his early career exploring ways to get to the root of the psychiatric conditions he was encountering in his practice.

Episode 21

RORSCHACH & FREUDIANS

MOVIE - Rorschach and the Freudians

Hysteria and Psychic Determinism

Hysteria is a condition in which psychological trauma or stress is converted into physical symptoms (this condition is called **conversion disorder** today). Freud concluded that ALL psychiatric conditions were the result of events that occurred earlier in life and that they could be resolved through the technique that he developed (**psychoanalysis**) which would result in a **catharsis event** (consider this to be sort of "ah ha" experience when we finally understand a question that has been bothering us).

The concept that early childhood experiences will manifest in symptoms later in life, a concept that we accept without question today, was termed **psychic determinism**. This thought of "determinism" would also manifest in Freud's psychosexual development model, as he felt that a person's personality was completely developed by the end of adolescence.

Instincts

Freud contended that humans had two basic instincts (though his conception of what constitutes an instinct is more in line with what we may call a "drive" or "impulse").

The first of these instincts is **Eros**, or the "life instinct". The energy of Eros was called **libido** (a term which is mistakenly associated with simple sexual energy). Consider this: Eros is our drive to survive, and libido is the energy we attach to making this happen. Early in life, we encountered individuals and objects in our world that were vital to our survival, to which we would attach libido energy.

We will see how the attachment of libido energy plays out in Freud's concept of attachment to objects and people and in Freud's developmental theory, where the libido becomes attached to a series of our own body parts.

Statue of Eros (at Piccadilly Circus, London), Son of Aphrodite and Ares (the Greek Gods of Love and War)
Eros is the image from which we come up with the character "Cupid"

Any problems, such as unsuccessful attachment with parents, abuse, neglect, sexual abuse, or simply a poor application of this energy was experienced as a threat to survival and led to problems later in life. This energy can become **fixated** at a developmental stage or on an object or person, leading to problems.

The other instinct that Freud identified with was the **death** instinct, which manifested with the energy of **aggression**. Freud did not pay as much attention to this particular instinct, and he felt it really only served to enable a person to defend him or herself in order to sustain the Eros, or life instinct.

Levels of Consciousness

One of the most profound, and still current, thoughts from Freud has to do with his levels of consciousness. Freud believed that most of our personality was actually hidden from our awareness in the **unconscious**. Access to these parts of our personality was only through what he called the **sub-** or **preconscious** which would serve

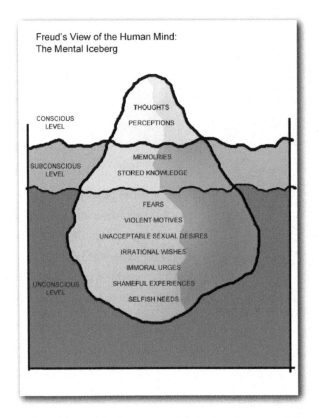

As you can see from this graphic, the content of the unconscious may not be acceptable and is, thus, suppressed. They, none-the-less, have an influence on us.

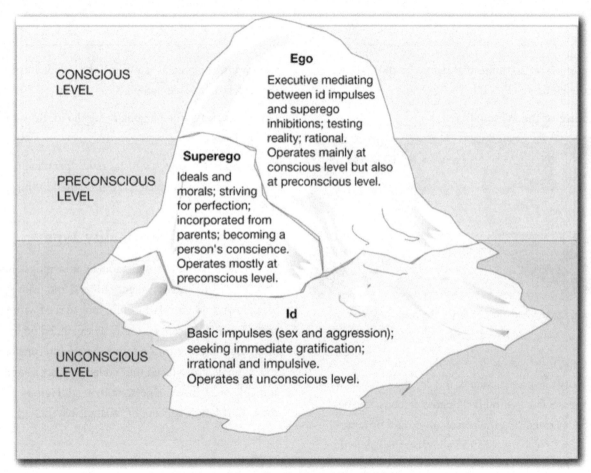

CONSCIOUS LEVEL

PRECONSCIOUS LEVEL

UNCONSCIOUS LEVEL

Ego

Executive mediating between id impulses and superego inhibitions; testing reality; rational. Operates mainly at conscious level but also at preconscious level.

Superego

Ideals and morals; striving for perfection; incorporated from parents; becoming a person's conscience. Operates mostly at preconscious level.

Id

Basic impulses (sex and aggression); seeking immediate gratification; irrational and impulsive. Operates at unconscious level.

Image from Psych Mental Health Hub

as a gate-keeper to things that would be allowed into the **conscious** state.

Structure of the Personality

The character Kronk from Disney's "Emperor's New Groove" has a moral decision to make!

Likely the most well-known of all of Freud's concepts is his theory on the structure of the personality, which is deeply associated with his thoughts on consciousness. Freud conceived that the personality could be represented as an iceberg. Most of an iceberg is below the surface of the water, as is most of the personality below the surface of consciousness.

The structures of the personalty are the **id**, the **ego**, and the **super-ego**.

Another popular way in which Freud's personality structure has been depicted is represented in this image!

Carl Jung and Personality Type

First, it is important to understand a few things about Carl Jung. Jung was a student of Freud and prior to a breakdown in their relationship, Jung agreed with much about Freud's concepts but greatly expanded on his thoughts about the unconscious, dream interpretation and symbols, introduced the "collective unconscious," and DID NOT invent a personality test! Here is a bit about Carl Jung's concept of "analytic psychology."

Basic Concepts of Analytic Psychology

Dynamic Psychic Energy

Jung felt that there was a dynamic exchange of energy between the conscious and unconscious parts of the personality. He generalized Freud's concept of the sexual energy (libido) into a more general "life force" that has been represented differently over the history of human kind.

Opposites

Jung suggested that much of nature is comprised of elements in opposition to one another. Keep in mind that Jung was influenced by Taoism and the concept of Yin and Yang, which also promote the idea of opposites in nature. In this world, the psyche seeks to find balance between all these opposing forces.

The Unconscious Mind

Similar to Freud's views, Jung believed that much of the personalty is unconscious, something he referred to as the **personal unconscious** to distinguish it from the shared nature of the **collective unconscious**. The collective unconscious is a reservoir of psychic resources common to all humans. These psychic resources are known as **archetypes**. These archetypes are passed on from generation to generation (and across the globe) through the collective unconscious.

Three significant archetypes, according to Jung, are:

1. **Shadow** - this is the inferior and least commendable aspects of a person. Consider it the source of our own personal "dark side".

2. **Anima** - the female part of the male psyche.

3. **Animus** - the male part of the female psyche.

Again we can recall the Yin Yang symbol from Japan.

According to Jung, there are many, many archetypes in the collective unconscious. The list in the textbook includes self, shadow, anima, animus, persona, hero, wise old man, and trickster.

We see these archetypes appear throughout historical literature and even in modern cinema and books. Complex story development reveals the anima and animus in the characters. Comic relief is provided by the trickster. Wise old men appear to advise the young, and heroes abound! These are universal themes across all cultures...it is no wonder that Jung came up with these ideas.

Symbols

Jung felt that some everyday objects may have hidden or representative meaning in the unconscious. For instance, in dream interpretation, the presence of a house has a literal meaning related to the building, but it also has a "hidden" meaning as representing the psyche. So, if the dreamer is wandering around the house trying to get into rooms, the interpretation might be that they are exploring hidden parts of their own mind!

The amazing thing about this field of study is how often different cultures come to the same conclusions about the meanings of symbols!

The white part represents male energy and the blackboard represents female energy...but notice that there is a little bit of male in the female and a little bit of female in the male...this is what is meant by the archetypes of the anima and animus.

Personality Types

One of the most famous personality tests is the Myers-Briggs Type Indicator (MBTI). What you may not know is that the MBTI was modeled after the theories of personality put forth by Carl Jung!

According to Jung, the personality is made up of an **attitude type** and four **function types:**

1. **Extroversion or introversion** (attitude type) - extroversion extends energy into the world around us, while introversion withdraws energy.

2. **Thinking or feeling** - thinking involves intellect and it tells you what something is; feelings, on the other hand, tell you what something is worth to you.

3. **Sensing or intuition** - sensing involves paying attention to the reality of your external environment, while intuition incorporates a sense of time and encompasses hunches.

MBTI

Katherine Briggs and her daughter, Isabel Briggs Myers, became fascinated with Jung's theories on personality and eventually added another dimension, **judging or perceiving**. Judging reflects a more controlled and planned out lifestyle, whereas perceiving is a more flexible and adaptive lifestyle.

The MBTI produces scores along 4 dimensions:

1. Introversion (I) vs. Extroversion (E)

2. Sensing (S) vs. Intuition (N)

3. Thinking (T) vs. Feeling (F)

4. Perceiving (P) vs. Judging (J)

The results produce a series of 4-letter sequences that correspond to a letter from each pair (as indicated above). One combination might be INTP another may be ENFJ. The total number of possible combinations is 16. These constitute the 16 personality types of Jung's theory!

ISTJ Responsible Executors	**ISFJ** Dedicated Stewards	**INFJ** Insightful Motivators	**INTJ** Visionary Strategists
ISTP Nimble Pragmatics	**ISFP** Practical Custodians	**INFP** Inspired Crusaders	**INTP** Expansive Analyzers
ESTP Dynamic Mavericks	**ESFP** Enthusiastic Improvisors	**ENFP** Impassioned Catalysts	**ENTP** Innovative Explorers
ESTJ Efficient Drivers	**ESFJ** Committed Builders	**ENFJ** Engaging Mobilizers	**ENTJ** Strategic Directors

Here is a great website about the 16 Personality Types

This is a fantastic version of the test with lots of interesting results for free. Of course, they will offer you paid resources to go deeper, but this is not expected. Email the results to yourself and then continue to read all the neat resources they provide for free.

Trait Theories and the Big 5

Quite different from the approaches to understanding personality that we have covered so far, trait theories attempt to identify psychological phenomena that allow some ability to predict the behavior of individuals.

Trait theories have arisen through the effort to identify the different patterns of human behavior that identify a person. Different theorists have taken very different approaches.

Personal Dispositions

Gordon Allport presented that there were collections of our traits grouped together in categories that indicated their importance in defining our personality.

Gordon Allport - Wikipedia

1. **Cardinal disposition** - this set of traits dominates throughout our lives. They cannot be hidden and the person is well known by them.

2. **Central disposition** - if you asked a good friend to describe someone, they would point out a number of central disposition traits in addition to the cardinal ones. These are the traits we might include in a letter of reference for someone.

3. **Secondary disposition** - these traits are less conspicuous, less stable, and less likely to be called into action.

Mature Personality

Allport also wrote about what constitutes a healthy adult personality. These might be akin to some of the traits we see in a self-actualized person (Maslow) or they may be pre-requisite personality traits for attaining self-actualization:

1. Extension of the sense of self

2. Warm relating of self to others

3. Emotional security (self acceptance)

4. Realistic perceptions, skills, and assignments

5. Self objectification - insight and humor

6. Unifying philosophy of life

Do you know of anyone who has the majority (or all) of these traits? I would bet they are pretty interesting people to have around!

Raymond Cattell and the 16PF

Despite his controversial views on eugenics, I have a connection to the work of Cattell that grew during my undergraduate years studying psychology.

While I attended St. Thomas University in Fredericton, NB, Canada, I was introduced to a psychologist by the name of John Gillis. Dr. Gillis, famous in his own right for his publication of the best-seller *Too Tall, Too Small,*

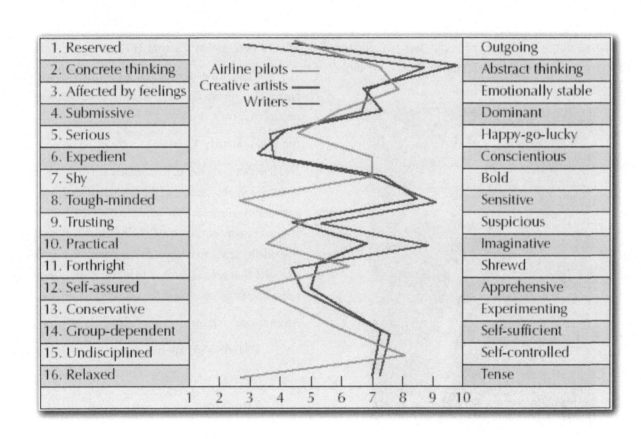

	1	2	3	4	5	6	7	8	9	10	
1. Reserved											Outgoing
2. Concrete thinking											Abstract thinking
3. Affected by feelings											Emotionally stable
4. Submissive											Dominant
5. Serious											Happy-go-lucky
6. Expedient											Conscientious
7. Shy											Bold
8. Tough-minded											Sensitive
9. Trusting											Suspicious
10. Practical											Imaginative
11. Forthright											Shrewd
12. Self-assured											Apprehensive
13. Conservative											Experimenting
14. Group-dependent											Self-sufficient
15. Undisciplined											Self-controlled
16. Relaxed											Tense

Airline pilots —
Creative artists —
Writers —

an analysis of the psychology of height, was the official biographer of Raymond Cattell (and published the biography titled *Psychology's Secret Genius*).

Raymond Cattell - Wikipedia

The 16 Personality Factors (PF)

The 16PF identifies scores along a continuum across 16 personality dimensions. Following, is an image of the results of a 16PF tests.

Big 5 Personality Traits

The five factor model of personality is currently the most widely recognized and established structure of personality. Researchers conducted a factor-analysis study on many of the established trait theory tests of personality and came upon a trend that identified 5 basic traits that are recognized in all the tests. These became known as the "big 5."

An easy way to remember the 5 traits...

1. Openness to experience
2. Conscientiousness
3. Extroversion
4. Agreeableness

5. Neuroticism

Note all the first letters spell OCEAN, so it is easier to remember!

Know Thyself

Psychology has made the personal study of our own personality a relatively easy task with an abundance of interesting and valid options for self testing.

There are many advantages to knowing more about yourself through self study.

Take the Big 5 Personality Test Online

Yes, you can be an outgoing introvert! Here are three signs you fit this personality profile.

MOVIE - Personality and why it Matters

Assessment

Chapter 11 Discussion - Freud

Freud is a controversial figure in the history of psychology. However, his contributions to our current understanding of personality, the nature of mental disease, and human development are still with us. Discuss ways in which Freud's work still has meaning in today's world of psychology

Chapter 11 Quiz

1. Complete the Big 5 Personality Test and report on you results. Reflect on the accuracy of this test and how the test might be useful to you.

Social Psychology

12

Attention

Perceptions of Beauty

One might think that "beauty" is a universal aspect of the human experience, and in some ways it is, but the consideration of what people find attractive in the looks of other people is largely culturally based. Different cultures find different physical traits to be "beautiful."

In media-centric areas of the world, the notion of "ideal beauty" has market value to sell products and services that promise that the ideal can be achieved. In the previous video, there are many examples of the use of cosmetics and plastic surgery to alter one's look to conform to a more idealistic standard.

One would think that we would not be fooled by the ads, but we are. In 2016, the U.S. market for cosmetics was $64 billion dollars. To understand the scale of this...if we stacked 1 billion dollars on top of one another, the tower would be 68 miles high.

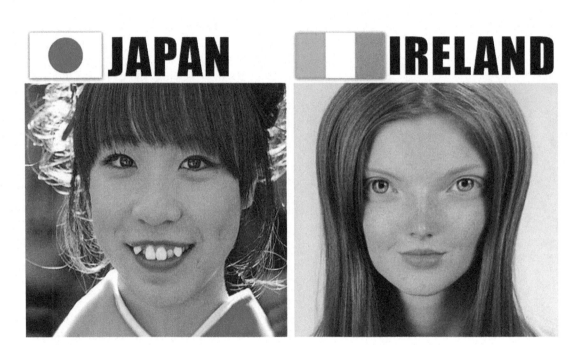

MOVIE - Beauty Standards in Different Countries in the World

That is a LOT of cosmetics...

1. A billion seconds ago, it was 1959.

2. A billion minutes ago, Jesus was alive.

3. A billion hours ago, our ancestors lived in caves.

4. A billion days ago, no one walked on two feet on Earth.

5. A billion dollars ago was only 8 hours and 20 minutes of government spending.

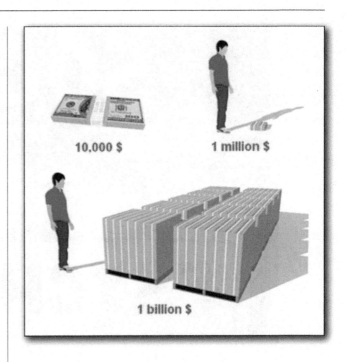

10,000 $ 1 million $

1 billion $

MOVIE - What is Social Psychology

Learning Outcomes

Upon completion of this chapter, students should be able to:

1. Discuss diverse experiences of role strain and role conflict.

2. Reflect on the personal reality of the looking glass self.

3. Discuss the concept of media used as a means of molding the mind of the public.

Teaching

The Power of the Situation

When I first encountered the world of psychology, I was frustrated by the inability of the science to predict behavior accurately. The one answer I repeated to many questions was, "well, it depends on...".

What ensued was a long list of factors that impact the probability of a specific behavioral response. While a lot of psychology focuses on individual factors, such as disposition, intelligence, perception, capacity to learn, etc., the field of social psychology focuses research on the factors that are external to the individual. Some of the factors that shape the way we behave are outside of us and can be found in our situations.

Consider a simple behavior (at least in our experience) of talking and your choice of words in a conversation. Consider how your choice of words to describe things would be different in each of these situations:

1. Alone with your best friend

If you were seated in this circle, how would you act? What if this were a group of friends, or a support group...sometimes the behaviors expected are actually outlined in rules to help us conform to the needs and purpose of the group.

2. With a group of friends and acquaintances

3. With your parents

4. With your grandparents

5. With a person who is interviewing you for a job you really want

6. When you are with a famous person you admire or look up to

It is easy to see how you would choose your words (and probably a lot of other behaviors) simply by analyzing the social situation in which you are acting!

Situational vs. Dispositional

In the world of social psychology, we define factors as either dispositional or situational. Dispositional factors are those that are a part of our unique selves. This includes a lot of what we have been talking about in this class up to this time: intelligence, personality, mood states, motivations, etc.

Situational factors are those that exist outside of ourselves in the environment around us. One of the fundamental advantages that humans have over animals is the ability to adapt to our surroundings, including our social situations. These factors are largely explored in the world of sociology. We will be drawing a lot of information from sociology in the material here.

Disposition and Internal vs. External Locus of Control

One interesting juxtaposition of both dispositional and situational factors is the concept of locus of control. Locus of control is an aspect of our personality that outlines our perceptions regarding our control and impact on our own lives. The upcoming graphic exemplifies the extremes of external and internal locus.

It is rare that any one individual is completely internal or external on all aspects of their lives, but it is clear that those with internal locus of control may, in fact, have more success at life than those who are primarily external. Take the test below to find out more about yourself!

Locus of Control and Attributional Style Test

Here is an example:

Billy is in school studying psychology. An exam is coming up but he has not really prepared as much as he should have. He takes the exam and performs badly. He notices, however, that some other students in the class seemed to have scored quite high on the exam.

We don't know what Billy's personality is but here are some ways that Billy could react to his poor performance that would give us some indicators:

1. *Billy justifies his poor score based his notion that the teacher failed to teach the material well.*

2. *Billy justifies his poor score based his notion that the material is too difficult for a simple Introduction to Psychology class.*

3. *Billy justifies his poor score based his notion that the professor shows favoritism to certain students in the class and scored his essays unfairly.*

Each of these perceptions would indicate to me that Billy has an external locus of control. He is attributing his failure to external factors. What if Billy reacted in one of these ways:

1. *Billy realizes he did not prepare adequately for the exam and deserves the score that he received.*

2. *Billy realizes that he has been prioritizing other recreational activities instead of studying.*

3. *Billy realizes that he will have to seek tutoring assistance and meet with the professor to improve his grades.*

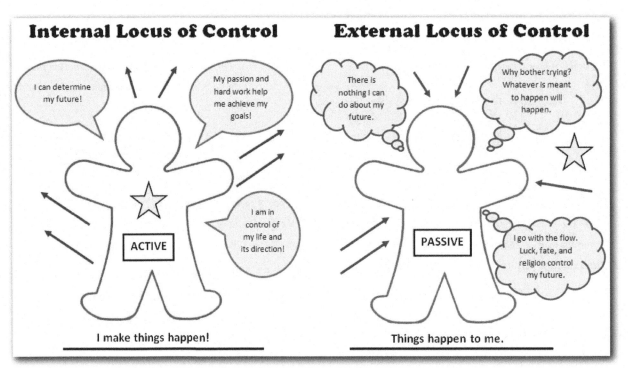

Image from simplepsychology.org

Each of these perceptions would indicate that Billy has an internal locus of control.

Fundamental Attribution Error

Included in the study of locus of control is our attributional style. It has been observed that many individuals have engaged in what is called the "fundamental attribution error."

Let's look at Billy's perceptions as to what we would "typically" see if someone was making the fundamental attribution error.

It is not uncommon for persons in Billy's situation to make the following errors:

1. *Personal success is credited as the result of internal characteristics.*

2. *Personal failure is credited as the result of external factors.*

3. *Others' success is credited as the result of external factors.*

4. *Others' failure is credited as the result of internal characteristics.*

Let's see how this would be expressed by Billy:

1. *If Billy did well on the test, he is likely to attribute this to internal characteristics such as his intelligence and hard work, rather than qualities of the test and teaching.*

2. *If Bill did poorly on the test, he is likely to attribute it to poor test construction and teaching.*

3. *If others did well (and particularly if he did not do well), Billy will likely attribute the success to cheating or being favored by the professor.*

4. *If others did poorly (and particularly if he did well), Billy will likely attribute the failure to others simply not being smart enough or being lazy.*

Consider situations that you have encountered like this. They may be in situations like the classroom, being in-

MOVIE - Fundamental Attribution Error

terviewed for a job, playing sports, etc. Can you remember committing the fundamental attribution error?

Social Structure and Psychology

In sociology, we identify that our culture and the social structures that we are surrounded with have a tremendous impact on our behavior.

Culture

Culture is to us like water is to fish. It surrounds us, penetrates us, and binds the galaxy together… wait, that's the Force!

But really, culture is all around us and defines our norms, values, and behavioral expectations from a family, group, even national perspective. What is "normal," as we will see when we study abnormal behavior later, may depend on which culture it occurs in!

Social Structure

Another aspect of culture is social structure. Consider this as a sort of organizational chart that identifies the job titles and job duties in a company…except, the company is our culture, and individuals within our culture can hold all sorts of jobs.

The job titles are called **statuses** and the job descriptions are called **roles**.

In a similar way, we all have multiple statuses and the roles that accompany them. These are connected to the **groups** that we belong to and define how others expect us to behave. Each of these groups is considered a **social group** with its own culture (norms, values, and expectations).

Role Strain and Role Conflict

Get ready for some really great content! The concepts of role strain and role conflict define "stress" from a sociological point of view! Let me explain.

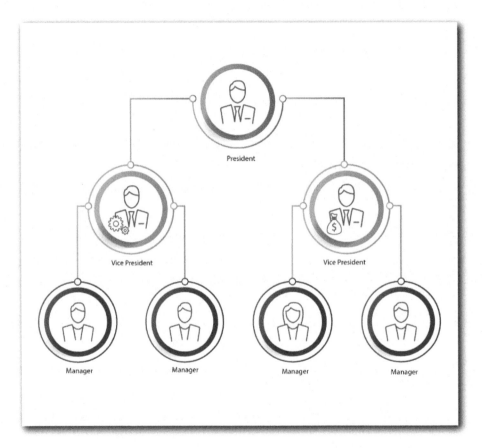

Consider this simple organizational chart for a company. It identifies specific statuses (I left out the roles) within the company and identifies the lines and manner of communication in a simple, graphic way.

In our modern world, we often have a multiplicity of statuses and for each status a "job description" entailing multiple roles. It stands to reason that sometimes these will not agree with one another!

When two "roles" are defined in such a way that it is **difficult** to do both of them, we call that **role strain**. My "family-husband-responsibilities in the household" role may be difficult to maintain alongside my "KVCC-professor-prepare for and teach classes" role. There are just so many hours in a day. So, when we take on roles that make it difficult to get everything done, we are experiencing role strain. I'm sure you have some compelling examples of this.

When two "roles" are defined in such a way that it is **impossible** to do both of them, we have a **role conflict**. My "family-husband-do activities with my wife" role is sometimes in conflict with my "band-bass play-play at gigs" role. My wife once bought tickets for us to go to a concert together, only to find that it conflicted with a band gig. I could only do one, not both.

Looking Glass Self

When I teach sociology one of my favorite topics to talk about is the theory of **looking glass self**. This theory

The Looking Glass Self

How my mom and dad see me.

How my girlfriend sees me.

How my older brother sees me.

How my ex-girlfriend sees me.

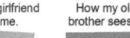

Type to enter text

was first presented by Charles Horton Cooley in 1902 and posits that a person's sense of self grows out of interactions with important people in our lives and our perceptions of how they view us and evaluate our performance. In short, a lot of who we are comes from others' views of who we are. Let me explain.

In the next image, you see a person looking at four mirrors (the old term for "mirror" is "looking glass"). The individual looks into the mirror and attempts to conceive how others in their lives look at them. In this example, the person perceives how his "mom and dad," "girlfriend," "older brother," and "ex-girlfriend" see him.

Each of these viewpoints are based upon the original person's understanding or assumptions about how the other people views them. These viewpoints are incorporated into the original person's sense of who they really are based on how important the others are in their lives.

So, part of our sense of self is built up by the perceptions we have of how other people perceive us!

The Looking Glass Committee

In my own teaching on this concept, I conceived the notion that we all have a "looking glass committee." These are individuals in our lives who have the power to influence our sense of self because we use their mirror to create our own sense of self.

These individuals can include family (who we did not choose), they can include friends (that we did choose), or they can include society at large (the mysterious "they" when we hear comments such as "what will they think about you?").

Let's say that the image above represents individuals in your life who are currently sitting on your committee. You are faced with a decision, so you think about whether or not this decision is in line with how these important people think about you and you get a vote from each one (in your mind).

As adults, we get to select who is on our committee, but some people, like our parents and other significant childhood adults can have a lasting impact on us. People don't even need to be alive to have a lasting impact on us! Consider the committee on the next page!

We may have a great set of committee members who are supportive of who we are, but if one person, perhaps a really important one (like a parent or teacher) is constantly disapproving of you, it can impact your sense of self dramatically.

Are there people on your committee like the woman in blue who you need to FIRE from their job on your committee? Why is this not easy to do sometimes?

Conformity and Social Control

Another aspect of sociology that impacts our behavior is the power of groups, and the fact that each group we belong to has an expectation that we conform and has a process of bringing us "back in line" with these expectations if we deviate from them.

The process by which, willingly or not, we go along with the group expectations is called **conformity**. Each group has a culture and within all cultures is a process by which the group enforces this conformity among its members. This process is called **social control**.

Written out that way, it sounds very bad, but if we WANT to be part of a group...let's say the United Bikers of Maine...there are some rules we need to follow (conformity) and if we break these rules, there may be some consequences (social control).

Conformity in the United Bikers of Maine

The United Bikers of Maine (UBM) is a motorcycle rights organization that supports motorcyclists and the love of riding motorcycles. Over the years of its existence, the UBM was primarily made up of individuals who not only ride motorcycles, but ride Harley Davidson motorcycles.

For a period of time, this created a divide among members who had a Harley and those who did not. At this time, the expectation is that respect will be shown to all members "regardless of the brand of motorcycle they ride."

Social Control in the United Bikers of Maine

The fee to join the UBM is $20 per year. If you fail to pay the fee, your membership with be terminated. The UBM also has a "biker down" support program for bikers involved in an accident. However, if the accident involved alcohol or other drugs, the biker is not eligible for services.

These rules provide structure and expectations of behavior to all members of the UBM.

Consider the groups that you belong to...KVCC, this course, your family, your country, clubs, organizations, employers...each of these have expectations for conformity and processes to encourage your conformity through social control.

Consumer Culture

The last topic I would like to explore is **consumer culture,** which is very prominent in the West. First, what do we mean by "consumer culture"?

Consumer culture can be broadly defined as a culture where social status, values, and activities are centered on the consumption of goods and services. One way to look at this might be to consider how much time in our day we spend **producing** versus how much time we spend in a day **consuming**.

Now before we go down too deep into this, we want to be sure that we are not judgmental about a person's passion for watching movies or reading or eating out a restaurants a lot. I just want to demonstrate that a lot of what we do is based on the consumption of something. In fact, if you want to follow this reasoning, a lot of our producing (work) is to earn money so we can consume (buy) things!

Compare the following different pictures of family possessions from different parts of the world.

The differences cannot be more stark. Again, this is not a condemnation of the concept of owning stuff, but it certainly highlights how much of what we do is centered around acquiring it.

The Father of Public Relations

This content was suggested by Jamie Landstam

Though famous in his own right, and profoundly wealthy due to the success he enjoyed in his work, he was also famous for being the nephew of none other than Sigmund Freud.

His uncle's work had a profound influence on Bernays' work. Bernays developed some of the most impactful aspects of the media that ushered in the consumer culture. Here are two examples of Bernays' work as he in-corporated the work of his uncle into the sale of products:

Torches of Freedom

In 1929, it was taboo for a woman to be smoking. If one did, they were often thought to be sexually promiscuous as well. The president of the Lucky Strike cigarette company hired Bernays to break the taboo so the company could expand their sales market to women.

Barnays consulted his uncle's work and interviewed psychoanalysts in New York City. When asking about what cigarettes mean to women, they replied that it symbolizes "male power."

Among other things, he organized an event that portrayed stylish women smoking cigarettes by convincing them it would serve women's equality. The success of this propaganda can be reviewed on the following site.

What Bernays had demonstrated is that his famous uncle was correct — irrational forces move people's behavior and if those could be connected to an idea (such as women's independence), people could be manipulated!

Bacon and Eggs

Around the same time, the typical American breakfast was a light one of juice, coffee, and toast. The Beechnut Packing Company wished to increase sales in the lagging bacon market (how can THAT be?) and hired Bernays to solve it.

Considering the problem, Bernays reasoned that individuals would trust their doctor to tell them about what to eat. So he hired doctors to suggest a hearty meal. Bacon and Eggs was born!

How Bacon and Eggs became the American Breakfast

While most of this is pretty trivial, it is important to understand what Bernays ushered in. Perhaps it is best to consider the words of the man himself from his book *Propaganda*:

"The conscious and intelligent manipulation of the organized habits and opinions of the masses is an important element in democratic society. Those who manipulate this unseen mechanism of society constitute an invisible government which is the true ruling power of our country. We are governed, our minds are molded, our tastes formed, and our ideas suggested, largely by men we have never heard of…It is they who pull the wires that control the public mind."

Bernays is largely responsible for the fact that cigarette companies successfully marketed smoking to women.

Torches of Freedom - Women and Smoking Propaganda

For more information on the work and influence of Bernays, visit this site.

The Birth of Manipulation with Edward Bernays

MOVIE - He said Cigarettes to Women are "Torches of Freedom"

Assessment

Chapter 12 Discussion - Society

"The conscious and intelligent manipulation of the organized habits and opinions of the masses is an important element in democratic society. Those who manipulate this unseen mechanism of society constitute an invisible government which is the true ruling power of our country. We are governed, our minds are molded, our tastes formed, and our ideas suggested, largely by men we have never heard of...It is they who pull the wires that control the public mind."

Discuss...

Chapter 12 Quiz

1. Each of us juggles multiple statuses and roles within our lives. Share specific instances of role strain and role conflict. Be sure to review the specific differences between these and make these differences clear in your answer.

2. Consider the different social groups that you belong to, each with its own culture and expectations for behavior. Describe a specific instance of what would happen if you engaged in some "deviance" and "broke a rule" in this group. Describe the group's informal and/or formal "social control" mechanisms.

Chapter 12 Assignment - Looking Glass Self

Purpose

This assignment has you examine your own social world through the theory of looking glass self. This theory posits that at all times during our lives we are subject to the judgement of a set of people. As adults, we have the opportunity to select who sits on this "committee" and the impact they have on our sense of self and identity.

By understanding the influence of specific people in our lives, we can better manage who we select for this important job and we can identify the specific source of certain aspects of our self concept.

Skills and Knowledge

You will demonstrate the following skills and knowledge by completing this assignment:

1. A thorough knowledge of the workings of the theory looking glass self

2. Identification of specific individuals within one's social world who act on us in accordance with the looking glass self

3. Identify the ways in which these individuals impact our sense of self

4. Identify current and historical changes that have been made, or could be made, to this "committee" and why

5. Write a paper in a word processor

6. Upload the paper to the appropriate assignment dropbox

Task

Review the concept of looking glass self in the Teaching section of this chapter. Reflect upon the individuals who have occupied seats on this "committee" in your past and in your current life. Who are these individuals, and which aspects of your self are they able to influence?

Reflect upon individuals who have had (or currently have) positions on this committee but have not been constructive aspects of your life. Reflect on why these individuals occupied this status in your life, why they are gone (or why they are still there), and how they have impacted you.

Write this paper using the following rubric and submit it to the appropriate dropbox.

Criteria for Success

Use the rubric below as a guide to this assignment:

Title Page   10 points

Standard title page with name, date, course, college name and the name of the assignment.

Looking Glass Self   20 points

Provide a definition of the theory in your own words.

Current   20 points

List current people on your "committee" and the specific aspect of your self that they have influence over.

Changes   20 points

Write an essay outlining specific changes in membership to this committee and how this came about.

Needs   20 points

Identify any needs you have to remove anyone from the committee and explore why this may be difficult or impossible.

Mechanics   10 points

Spelling, syntax, and organizational structure of the paper. Clear and organized.

I-O Psychology

13

Attention

Why does Apple use a Trashcan and Windows uses a Recycle Bin?

Human factors psychology and human factors engineering (sub-categories of industrial-organizational psychology) have played a very important role in our lives. These scientists and engineers produce the interfaces that we use every day with our computers and our portable devices.

In the early days of computing, there was no such thing as a graphic user interface (GUI - pronounced Gewey). People interacted with computers through buttons and knobs (and later punch cards). Modern computers use analogies of the real world so that users are better able to understand how to use them.

Check out the following images of the original GUIs for Apple and Windows computers and the linked article on the history of the GUI!

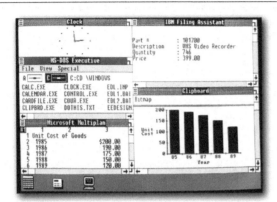

Windows 1.0

Mac OS 1.0

A Short History of Computer User Interface Design

Learning Outcomes

Upon completion of this chapter, students should be able to:

1. Apply Gilbert's behavioral engineering model.

2. Discuss personal examples of both formal and informal work culture.

Teaching

Psychology in the Workplace

Considering the amount of time we spend preparing for, and actually working in, our jobs, it stands to reason that psychology would be interested in studying it. **Industrial-organizational psychology** (I-O psychology) combines the fields of industrial and organizational psychology to study how human behavior and psychology effect work and how people are affected by work.

Industrial psychology focuses on the hiring and maintenance of employees, whereas organizational psychology focuses on employee relationships and organizational culture. These areas of interest are distinct but definitively intertwined in an organization.

Origins of I-O Psychology

Because I-O psychology shares a lot of interest with sociology and social psychology, its origins are similar. All three arose primarily around the advent of the European and American Industrial Revolutions, advertising, and around the great wars, World War I and World War II.

It was these circumstances that demanded that we develop an understanding of how people work in groups, how to select the best persons for different jobs, how to convince people to buy the products that we are making, and how to keep workers productive even under stressful conditions. Accomplishments and discoveries during this early time include:

1. Cataloging of military jobs and alignment with skills and characteristics (which ushered in the development of the Armed Services Vocational Aptitude Battery)

2. Research around environmental factors such as lighting and temperature on worker productivity

3. The study of leadership styles, team structure, and group dynamics in the workplace by Kurt Lewin in the 1930s

4. The Army Alpha (verbal) and Army Beta (nonverbal) intelligence testing instruments

Frederick Taylor

In 1911, Taylor published *The Principles of Scientific Management*.

Although this work was highly criticized for having little concern for worker's well being, the principles outlined in this seminal work are still implemented today.

The book addresses management styles, personnel selection and training, and work itself (using timing and motion studies).

The ultimate goal of this type of work was to maximize worker productivity. Some of the concepts that endure into the modern age from this work include:

1. Scheduled break times

2. Arrangement of materials on an assembly line

3. Time studies on work productivity

4. Machines that were built to be more comfortable for humans to operate

5. Ergonomics

Lillian and Frank Gilbreth

The Gilbreths, husband and wife, conducted studies on efficiency in the workplace. They worked to develop ways to reduce the number of motions required to complete a task, thus increasing productivity. They also studied worker stress and motivation (finding that indeed, many employees are motivated by money and job satisfaction).

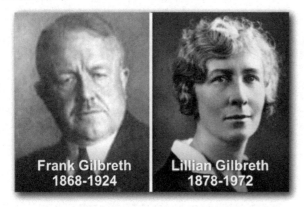

Frank Gilbreth
1868-1924

Lillian Gilbreth
1878-1972

Lillian Gilbreth, an engineer, is also credited with the notion of placing a foot pedal to open the lid of a trash can and the idea of putting shelves on the door of a refrigerator!

Thomas Gilbert

Thomas Gilbert was a psychologist who is often credited with creating the field of performance technology. He is best known for his book *Human Competence: Engineering Worthy Performance*. Gilbert was a student of BF Skinner and adapted the A-B-C Contingency Model of operant conditioning to the workplace.

In his book, Gilbert introduces the formula for "worthy performance":

$$\frac{\text{Accomplishment}}{\text{Behavior}}$$

This formula posits that if the cost of the behavior exceeds the value of the accomplishment (if someone is paid too much for what they get done), this fails to be worthy performance.

Gilbert's Behavioral Engineering Model

	Information	Instrumentation	Motivation	
Environment	**1. Expectations & Feedback** • Does the individual know what is expected of them? • Do people know how well they're performing? • Are people given guidance about their performance?	**2. Tools & Resources** • Do people have the right tools for performance? • Are tools and materials designed to match the human factors of performance? Type to enter text	**3. Incentives (Consequences & Rewards)** • Are adequate financial incentives that are contingent upon performance available? • Are non-monetary incentives available? • Are career development opportunities available?	**Management System**
Individual	**4. Skills & Knowledge** • Do people have the skills and the knowledge needed to perform as expected? • Is well-designed training that matches the performance requirements available?	**5. Individual Capacity** • Is performance scheduled for times when people are at their best? • Do people have the aptitude and physical ability to perform the job?	**6. Motivation** • Are people willing to work for the incentives? • Are people recruited to match the realities of the job?	

All 6 conditions are equally important, and must be present for performance to occur.

Gilbert's Behavioral Engineering Model (adapted from Deb Wagner's HPT Toolkit)

Another contribution of Gilbert to our understanding of work is the behavior engineering model. This model proposes that in order to achieve maximum worthy performance, management must address both the work environment and the selection of the best worker for the job. The following table is used to "diagnose" areas that may interfere with performance.

Industrial Psychology

Industrial psychology focuses on the selection and training of employees. Any employer knows that they want the most qualified and competent person doing the job, so selection of the right person is vital.

Contributions to this end that have evolved out of industrial psychology include:

1. Job analysis - clear and accurate descriptions of all aspects of a given work in order to match candidates to the job and to advise accommodations under the Americans with Disabilities Act

2. Candidate testing

3. Interview processes

4. Training - specific educational processes to provide employees with the skills they need to do their work and/or to adapt to changes in their work

5. Performance evaluations processes

Three Very Important sets of Laws

While employers may wish to have the most qualified candidates fill empty positions in their organizations, bias on the part of the employer can be, and usually is, present. Persons of color, persons with disabilities, and women have advocated for years for laws to protect them from these biases.

Americans with Disabilities Act (ADA)

Passed in 1990, the ADA makes it illegal to discriminate against people based on their disability. The law also mandates "reasonable accommodations" for persons in the workplace. This is where an accurate job analysis is important. These reports identify the physical, mental, and emotional aspects of a job and separate "essential" duties from "non-essential duties."

Visit this page to read an overview of the ADA

Normally, accommodations apply only to non-essential duties. Technological innovation, however, has made it possible for persons with disabilities to engage in many work-related tasks. For example:

Sally suffered a spinal cord injury while skiing that affected all of her limbs. She has no ability to move her legs and has lost most fine-motor control of her upper limbs. She uses a wheelchair with a joystick motor operation for mobility. Prior to her accident, Sally was an accountant in a small tax firm. Wishing to return to work, she approached her employer about accommodating her workplace for her disabilities.

It was determined, for example, that Sally had to be able to enter the building on her own and she had to be able to enter data into a computer. Entering the building is considered to be a non-essential part of her job because it is not specific to her accounting job description, it is specific to the building. The law mandates that the employer explore reasonable ways to provide Sally with access to the building. The employer elects to build a ramp and automatic door opener so Sally can enter the building independently.

Entering data into the computer is determined to be an essential aspect of Sally's duties as an accountant. Without modern devices, Sally would not necessarily be eligible for accommodations for inability to type. Luckily, computer technology has advanced so that keyboards with different kinds of keys and even voice activated systems could be installed on her workstation that would allow her to enter data. The employer, again, willfully has the new software installed and Sally is able to return to her job.

Civil Rights Act and the Age Discrimination in Employment Act

Click here to review a whole set of court cases regarding the ADA

These laws protect individuals from suffering discrimination based on race, ethnicity, religion, gender, sexual orientation, and age. It also provides for the concept of **bona fide occupational qualifications** that allow employers to "discriminate" because of specific aspects of the job.

All of these laws are supported under civil law, therefore there is no "policing" of the law; organizations are expected to comply with these expectations. Individuals who feel they have been discriminated against must pursue legal action. Many states have laws and programs to assist individuals in these circumstances.

Organizational Psychology

Organizational psychology has a focus on the social and cultural aspects of the workplace and how interactions impact the workplace. Contributions from the world of organizational psychology include:

1. A focus on job satisfaction, employee health and wellness, and successful business

2. Work-family balance

3. Management and organizational structure - analysis of the ways in which decisions are made

and how individuals fit within the larger organization

4. Leadership styles

5. Teamwork factors

6. Addressing workplace violence and abuse

7. Organizational culture

Formal and Informal Organizational Culture

Organizational or work culture is essentially the term we used to describe all of the beliefs, attitudes, policies, and principles of the workplace. However, there are usually two kinds of work cultures at every organization, formal and informal.

Formal Work Culture

When you get a new job, or even when you became a student at KVCC, you were given an "orientation" as to "how things work" and what to expect.

This orientation is usually filled with a lot of information related to the roles of different people, how to accomplish certain tasks, and the "rules and policies" that are written in various manuals (such as an employee manual or even the Student Code of Conduct at KVCC).

This "formal" set of expectations represents the formal work culture of the organization. It is usually taught in the orientation and we sometimes receive written copies of it.

Informal Work Culture

In every organization there is also an "informal" work culture. This is the "insider" information as to how things "really work" at the job or in the company.

This information can be very important for someone to survive and thrive in the workplace, but it is hardly every included in the official orientation!

People learn the informal work culture through social connections in the workplace. These are the water cooler conversations where important information is passed on from employee to employee. When you make social connections at work, you learn the informal work culture through an informal process!

Assessment

Chapter 13 Discussion - Behavioral Engineering Model

Review Gilbert's behavioral engineering model. Consider a situation in which you have struggled to get a job done. Identify areas related in the model as to what could have been done to help you complete that task.

Chapter 13 Quiz - Cultures

1. Think of any work situation that you have been in and provide a brief description of an example of formal culture.

2. Think of any work situation that you have been in and provide a brief description of an example of informal culture.

Stress, Lifestyle, and Health

14

Attention

Positive Psychology and Happiness

While different people define happiness in different ways, it is likely that this is a state of being that nearly every human being on Earth is pursuing. But what is happiness, according to the field of psychology?

It seems there is a sort of "formula" to shoot for. Effectively a good, pleasant, and meaningful life.

Positive Psychology

Positive psychology is a sub-field in psychology that attempts to examine the condition of happiness and well-being. Psychology has a long history of focusing on "problems" and when things go "wrong" (This is understandable because that is where the money comes from...hardly anyone goes to see a psychologist when they are feeling great!).

Modern positive psychology is being led by the research of Martin Seligman and Mihály Csíkszentmihályi. Some of the topics studied in the field of positive psychology include:

1. Optimism
2. Altruism
3. Empathy
4. Creativity
5. Forgiveness
6. Compassion

Flow

The concept of flow was put forth by Mihály Csíkszentmihályi. Flow describes having an experience that is so engaging and engrossing that it becomes worth doing for its own sake (without external rewards or specific gain.) Creative types experience this state of mind when they are engrossed for periods of time in their work, either on a canvas, a typewriter, or on stage.

However, all of us that get deeply engrossed in a task can experience flow. The tendency is to lose track of time, effortless maintenance of concentration, and deep focus on the task. Some experiences of flow can be akin to the "peak experiences" that Maslow refers to in his discussion of the hierarchy of needs; experiences that are necessary to achieve "transcendence" and to become "self-actualized."

Flow has been found to be very much associated with measures of happiness. Csíkszentmihályi felt that creating conditions that made more experiences of flow possible should be a top social and political priority.

How might you make room for the possibility of more experiences of flow in your life?

Meaningful life
Contributing to the greater good

Good life
Using skills for enrichment

Happiness

Pleasant life
Enjoying daily pleasures

Learning Outcomes

Upon completion of this chapter, students should be able to:

1. Evaluate personal levels of stress using the Life Changes Stress Test.

2. Discuss examples of coping techniques including problem- and emotion-focused coping, control, social supports, and stress reduction techniques.

Teaching

Stressed?

In Chapter 12, we discussed stress from a sociological perspective by identifying degrees of role strain and stress. In this chapter, we are going to examine the concept of stress and how we determine the degree to which some sort of stimulus (either a charging rhino or another challenging assignment) is stressful.

A lot of things are stressful...if you THINK about it!

Although there are certain stimuli that will bring about a "flight or fight" response without a whole lot of thought (suddenly losing your balance, someone hitting you, etc.), there is actually a lot of THOUGHT that goes into determining if a stimulus is a stressor and how you are going to handle it. We engage in an **appraisal** of the situation, as described here in the graphic.

As you can see, how we interpret a particular stimulus or event largely determines if we are going to experience stress. Although, it is clear that even situations

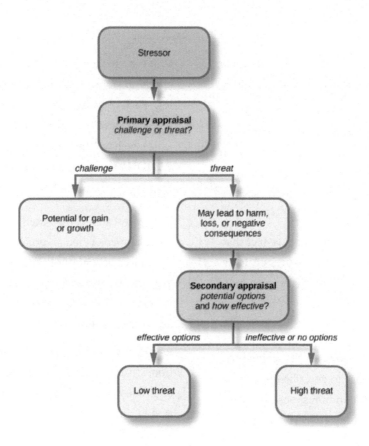

Image from lumenlearning.com

that present as potential for growth or gain can still be stressful due to performance concerns, fear of failure, and external expectations.

Stress that is connected to potential gain and growth is called **eusress** (from the Greek "eu" for "good"...as in euphoric). Situations such as planning a party, buying a new car, and having a child are usually "good" situations but they do entail the experience of "stress."

Consider different experiences that you have had that could be categorized as "stress" and "eustress." How did you experience the stress differently because of this appraisal?

Walter Cannon

Cannon was the Harvard physiologist who coined the term "fight-or-flight" response to describe the actions of the sympathetic nervous system in response to a significant stressor. To understand this process, let's take a look at the nervous system again.

When we perceive a threat, along with our cognitive appraisal, some very rapid changes happen in our bodies. Each of us has probably experienced this feeling when we have been thrust into scary situations. Sometimes we have these physiological reactions in ANTICIPATION of an upcoming situation!

Hans Selye

Selye's research contributed to our understanding about what happens when an organism is exposed to stressors over a long duration of time. Consider dangerous jobs, wartime experiences, and other long-term "stressful" situations. Selye described this process as **general adaptation syndrome**.

Essentially when we encounter a fight-or-flight situation, we are in the alarm reaction stage, and if the stress continues, we enter into a resistance phase. After a period of time, we become exhausted due to being in the fight-or-flight state for too long. Our "tiredness" can express itself through being sleepy, unmotivated, lethargic, and depressed. As covered elsewhere in our textbook, this continued situation has a great impact on our immune system as well.

Crisis Fatigue

Crisis Fatigue

In our current time, there is an overwhelming amount of crisis going on around the world. Earlier, we talked about negativity bias and availability heuristics as part of how the media is feeding into a sense of crisis, but none-the-less, there are real events, real troubles, and real worries going on.

Stress Management

Since both stress and eustress events cause us the same physiological issues, good and effective stress management is vital to living in our modern world.

Coping Styles

Each of us has learned to cope with stress in different ways. We have also adapted ways based upon our experiences. Here are some ways in which we cope with stress:

1. Problem-focused coping - attempts to manage or alter the conditions that are stressful

2. Emotion-focused coping - attempts to change or reduce the negative emotions associated with stress

Psychologists have long considered that the appropriate application of these coping strategies can be very effective. Knowing which circumstances require specific strategies is key to their effectiveness.

The self-help movement has long focused on making personal change and on learning to distinguish when and what you can change. Consider the following phrases that arise from the 12-step recovery models:

"God, grant me...
the serenity, to accept the things I cannot change
the courage, to change the things I can, and...
the wisdom, to know the difference!"

"Fake it 'till you make it!"

Other Aspects of Stress Management

The following is a list of some additional aspects of stress management that have an immense impact on our ability to be resilient in face of stress:

1. **Control** - Researchers repeatedly identify that our perceptions of control over our situation is a large part of stress management. This is related to our wish for "wisdom" so we can successfully identify where our control is!

2. **Social Supports** - Social support can manifest in many ways in our lives. Social connectedness has been heavily researched and associated with happiness, longevity, health and wellness, personal satisfaction, positive mental health, and successful aging.

3. **Stress Reduction Techniques** - Since there are both cognitive and physiological aspects of stress, there are both cognitive and physiological methods for reducing stress. Therapies such as cognitive restructuring and cognitive behavior therapy (CBT) focus on changing our seemingly automatic "thinking" about threats in our lives. Physiological ways to deal with stress include relaxation, meditation, exercise, and being in natural settings.

Each of us, of course, has developed different ways to cope with stress. Some of these are effective and good for us (exercise and listening to music) while others may be more damaging (yelling at others and lashing out). Learning to control our emotions is part of what we have already studied in the field of emotional intelligence. Here, again, we see how intertwined different areas of psychology are when the development of emotional intelligence can be seen as a very effective stress management tool.

What is Resilience? Psychologists explain how to grow from Painful Moments.

Assessment

Chapter 14 Discussion - Stress

Visit the American Institute of Stress and complete the Holmes-Rahe Stress Inventory. You will need to print out the PDF version of the test and complete it that way.

Report your score and discuss two events that contributed to your current stress score. Provide a brief description and evaluation of the methods you have been using for stress management.

How does the concept of crisis fatigue play into this?

Psychological Disorders

15

Attention

The Psychological Disorders According to Crash Course

Of all the categories of psychological information, Crash Course has the most videos on different psychological disorders. By way of introduction to all of these I have included links to each of them, in order, so you can familiarize yourself with these diagnoses.

Episode 28

PSYCHOLOGICAL DISORDERS

MOVIE - Psychological Disorders

Episode 29

OCD & ANXIETY DISORDERS

MOVIE - OCD & Anxiety

Episode 31

TRAUMA & ADDICTION

MOVIE - Trauma & Addiction

Episode 30

DEPRESSIVE & BIPOLAR DISORDERS

MOVIE - Depressive & Bipolar Disorder

Episode 32

SCHIZOPHRENIA & DISSOCIATIVE DISORDERS

MOVIE - Schizophrenia & Dissociative Disorders

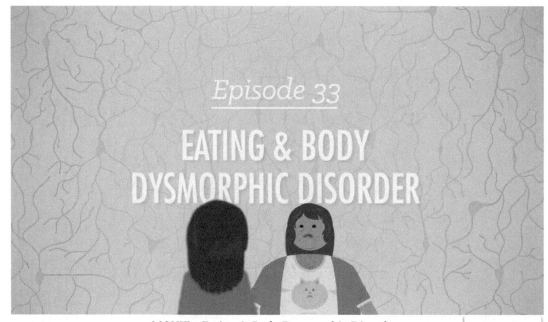

Episode 33

EATING & BODY DYSMORPHIC DISORDER

MOVIE - Eating & Body Dysmorphic Disorders

Episode 34

PERSONALITY DISORDERS

MOVIE - Personality Disorders

Learning Outcomes

Upon completion of this chapter, students should be able to:

1. Define the three criteria for determining if a behavior is abnormal.

2. Discuss the modern biological and psychological perspectives on the origin of psychological disorders.

3. Describe the symptoms, types, causes, and treatments of a selected mental disorder.

Teaching

What is Normal?

There can be no discussion about **abnormal** without a discussion about **normal**! Since there is such wide diversity as to what **normal** means, it is actually easier to define it by describing what it is NOT (abnormal).

In the field of psychology, which is very oriented toward understanding abnormal behavior, there are three areas that we need to examine to determine if a behavior is to be considered **abnormal**.

Statistics

When someone acts in a way that strikes you as "abnormal" it does so because it is unusual, it stands out, and it rarely happens. If this were not the case, then it would not strike you as abnormal; it would be normal! The notion is that MOST people do not do abnormal things, because then they would be called normal.

My point is this, one test to determine if behavior is abnormal is asking the question: "Is it rare?" For this, we

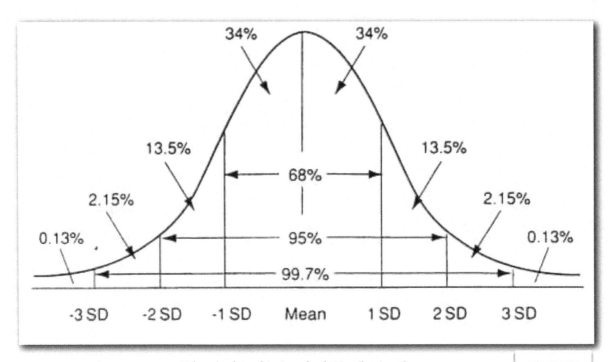

Take a look at this Standard Distribution Curve

are going to us a very commonly known graph called the standard distribution curve.

As you learned in the previous video, observations of many things in the world that are either really above or below the mean are rare. In order for a behavior to be considered abnormal, it should only be observed in a small percentage of the population, +/- 2 standard deviations. Looking at the graph, you would identify the middle line that says 95%. This means that 95% of people do not show this extreme of behavior, the 5% (2.5% higher and 2.5% lower) represent the "abnormal" behavior. So, our first criteria is: in order for the behavior to be considered abnormal, it needs to be rare.

Culture

When I introduced Chapter 12, the concept of cultural norms, values, and expectations was discussed. All of our cultures have "norms" for our behavior. This manifests itself in all our groups and societies. We have norms associated with our family culture (eating dinner together, no cell phones at the table, etc.), we have norms associated with school (attend class, do homework, ask questions), and we have norms in our larger society (drive at posted speed limits, don't steal things, treat others with respect).

So, culture comes into play in determining if a behavior is abnormal. Abnormal behaviors in society are dealt with as either "criminal" or "illness" based. Abnormal behavior that is considered "criminal" is dealt with by the Criminal Justice System, and abnormal behavior that is considered "illness based" is dealt with by the mental health system (and yes, sometimes it is both!).

Function

Lastly we have Function. This criteria refers to the ability of an individual to engage in the activities of life including: self-care, relationships, work, recreation, etc. A behavior is considered abnormal in this regard if it interferes with, or prevents, the person from engaging in these activities of life.

MOVIE - The Secret Life of Social Norms

This is a great TED event about the difference between "tight" and "loose" social norms

Chronic, Pervasive, and Persistent Mental Illness

Many of the mental disorders that are most commonly known (such as those introduced in the Attention section of this chapter) manifest in their most severe sense as chronic, pervasive, and persistent mental illness.

1. Chronic - this characteristic refers to the fact that the symptoms have been experienced for a very long time

2. Pervasive - this characteristic refers to the fact that many of the person's activities of life are deeply impacted

3. Persistent - this characteristic refers to the fact that symptoms resist treatment and/or are cyclical in nature

Persons with this level of mental disorder are often "disabled" and require intense levels of service. We will be discussing the application of psychosocial rehabilitation for this population in the next chapter.

Etiology of Mental Illness and Mental Disorders

Etiology is just a fancy word for "causes" or "origins"... thus, this section will discuss the modern understanding of the causes of mental disorders. Modern perspectives vary dramatically from historical perspectives from the supernatural to weakness of the will. The website below provides an interesting summary of these perspectives.

History of Mental Illness - Noba Psychology

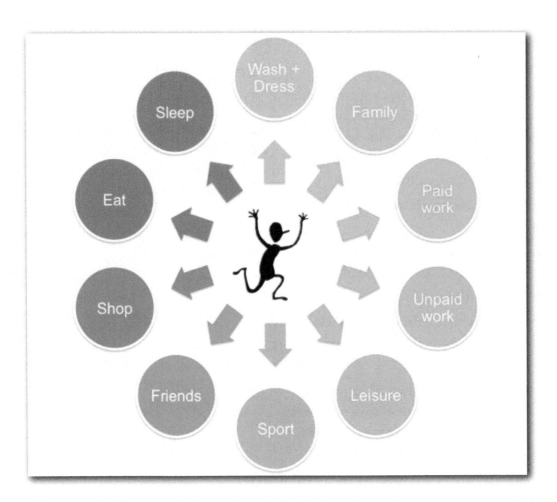

Modern perspectives on the origin of mental illness describe two major areas:

Biological Perspective

The biological perspective of mental illness attributes the symptoms to genetic abnormalities, chemical imbalances, and abnormal brain structure. Contrary to many other perspectives, the resulting behavior, however willful it may seem, is the result of biological forces and the individual has very little ability to control them.

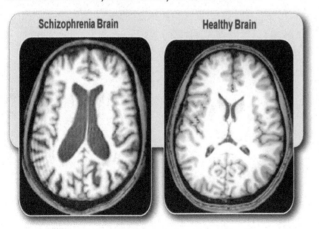

Although the results are not conclusive, many persons with schizophrenia have enlarged ventricles in their brains. Ventricles are spaces within the brain filled with cerebrospinal fluid that maintain the correct amount and pressure of fluid in the brain and spinal cord.

In the next chapter, we will be discussing the treatment protocols for medications and brain surgery as interventions that are embodied in the biological perspective.

Diathesis-Stress (DS) Perspective

While still taking into consideration the biological perspective, the DS approach validates the importance of learning, stress, faulty thinking, and environment as important determinants of mental functioning.

This model proposes that individuals with the predisposition for mental illness due to some biological mechanism are more at risk of actually developing a mental illness when they are compromised by psychosocial factors such as poverty, drugs, violence, poor decision making, low education attainment, etc.

Categorization of Mental Illness

As diverse as our brains are, the ways in which things can go wrong are numerous. Over the years, the fields of psychology and psychiatry continually attempt to define and describe the various mental disorders. The published work that is the most widely used guide to diagnostics is the **Diagnostic and Statistical Manual of Mental Disorders (DSM)** published by the American Psychiatric Association.

The current edition, DSM-5, is organized to provide the following information:

1. Diagnostic classifications
2. Diagnostic criteria sets
3. Descriptive text

The point of the DSM-5 is to provide a guide for clinicians to engage in **differential diagnosis,** which is the gathering of historical and current information on the patient's life in order to arrive at a diagnoses that cor-rectly identifies their disorder and to provide options for clinical interventions.

History of the DSM

Assessment

Chapter 15 Discussion - Mental Illness

Review the information on the current biological and psychosocial perspectives on the origins of mental illness. How do these compare to historical perspectives. Complete an internet search and discover/report on an example of bizarre and even barbaric practice from the past.

Do you think that people in the distant future will look back on our efforts with the same opinions?

Chapter 15 Quiz

1. Define the three criteria for determining if a behavior is abnormal.

Therapy and Treatment

16

Attention

Not all "help" was alway "helpful"

From *The Body* by Bill Bryson.

The Tragic History of Lobotomies

"In the 1880s, in a series of operations, a Swiss physician named Gottlieb Burckhardt surgically removed eighteen grams of brain from a disturbed woman, in the process turning her (in his own words) from 'a dangerous and excited demented person to a quiet demented one.' He tried the process on five more patients, but three died and two developed epilepsy, so he gave up. Fifty years later, in Portugal, a professor of neurology at the University of Lisbon, Egas Moniz, decided to try again and began experimentally cutting the frontal lobes of schizophrenics to see if that might quiet their troubled minds. It was the invention of the frontal lobotomy (though it was then often called a leukotomy, particularly in Britain).

"Moniz provided an almost perfect demonstration of how not to do science. He undertook operations without having any idea what damage they might do or what the outcomes would be. He conducted no preliminary experiments on animals. He didn't select his patients with particular care and didn't monitor outcomes closely afterward. He didn't actually perform any of the surgeries himself, but supervised his juniors -- though freely took credit for any successes. The practice did actually work up to a point. People with lobotomies generally became less violent and more tractable, but they also routinely suffered massive, irreversible loss of personality. Despite the many shortcomings of the procedure and Moniz's lamentable clinical standards, he was feted around the world and in 1949 received the ultimate accolade of a Nobel Prize.

"In the United States, a doctor named Walter Jackson Freeman heard of Moniz's procedure and became his most enthusiastic acolyte. Over a period of almost forty years, Freeman traveled the country performing lobotomies on almost anyone brought before him. On one tour, he lobotomized 225 people in twelve days. Some of his patients were as young as four years old. He operated on people with phobias, on drunks picked up off the street, on people convicted of homosexual acts -- on anyone, in short with almost any kind of perceived mental or social aberration. Freeman's method was so swift and brutal that it made other doctors recoil. He inserted a standard household ice pick into the brain through the eye socket, tapping it through the skull bone with a hammer, then wriggled it vigorously to sever neural connections. Here is his breezy description of the procedure in a letter to his son:

I have been...knocking them out with a shock and while they are under the "anesthetic" thrusting an ice pick up between the eyeball and the eyelid through the roof of the orbit actually into the frontal lobe of the brain and making the lateral cut by swinging the thing from side to side.

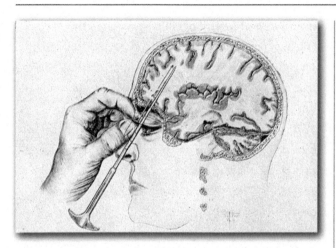

A drawing from Dr. Walter Freeman's book, Psychosurgery in the Treatment of Mental Disorders and Intractable Pain, shows his icepick-inspired transorbital lobotomy instrument.

Image from nihrecord.nih.gov

I have done two patients on both sides and another on one side without running into any complications, except a very black eye in one case. There may be trouble later on but it seemed fairly easy, although definitely a disagreeable thing to watch.

"Indeed. The procedure was so crude that an experienced neurologist from New York University fainted while watching a Freeman operation. But it was quick; patients generally could go home within an hour. It was this quickness and simplicity that dazzled many in the medical community. Freeman was extraordinarily casual in his approach. He operated without gloves or a surgical mask, usually in street clothes. The method caused no scarring but also meant that he was operating blind without any certainty about which mental capacities he was destroying. Because ice picks were not designed for brain surgery, sometimes they would break off inside the patient's head and have to be surgically removed, if they didn't kill the patient first. Eventually, Freeman devised a specialized instrument for the procedure, but it was essentially just a more robust ice pick.

"What is perhaps most remarkable is that Freeman was a psychiatrist with no surgical certification, a fact that horrified many other physicians. About two-thirds of Freeman's subjects received no benefit from the procedure or were worse off. Two percent died. His most notorious failure was Rosemary Kennedy, sister of the future president. In 1941, she was twenty-three years old, a vivacious and attractive girl but headstrong and with a tendency to mood swings. She also had some learning difficulties, though these seem not to have been nearly as severe and disabling as has sometimes been reported. Her father, exasperated by her willfulness, had her lobotomized by Freeman without consulting his wife. The lobotomy essentially destroyed Rosemary. She spent the next sixty-four years in a care home in the Midwest, unable to speak, incontinent, and bereft of personality. Her loving mother did not visit her for twenty years.

"Gradually, as it became evident that Freeman and others like him were leaving trails of human wreckage behind them, the procedure fell out of fashion, especially with the development of effective psychoactive drugs. Freeman continued to perform lobotomies well into his seventies before finally retiring in 1967. But the effects that he and others left in their wake lasted for years. I can speak with some experience here. In the early 1970s, I worked for two years at a psychiatric hospital outside London where one ward was occupied in large part by people who had been lobotomized in the 1940s and 1950s. They were, almost without exception, obedient, lifeless shells."

Learning Outcomes

Upon completion of this chapter, students should be able to:

1. Discuss the barriers to help-seeking.

2. Distinguish between treatment and rehabilitation.

3. Describe the symptoms, types, causes, and treatments of a selected mental disorder.

Teaching

May I help you?

Much of the modern world of psychology is focused on the helping profession. While much of this "help" is in the form of counseling and psychotherapy, nearly all aspects of psychology have goals to make the world a better place:

1. Educational psychologists want to help improve teaching and learning.

2. Social psychologists want to help individuals deal with social demands.

3. Industrial psychologists want to help organizations be productive.

4. Sports psychologists want to help players stay healthy and perform their best.

5. Clinical psychologists want to help people overcome their mental health issues and have a fulfilling life.

Episode 35

GETTING HELP

MOVIE - CrashCourse Psychology - Getting Help

The field of psychology has long applied its four goals to helping:

1. Describe

2. Explain

3. Predict

4. Control

Psychologists seek to describe the specific situation, explain the relationships between the variables, and predict how the outcomes would change if the variables changed. Interventions seek to **control** the particulars of a situation and make it better. However, this can rarely be done successfully without the full commitment and dedication of the persons involved.

Barriers to Getting Help

The following information comes from a comprehensive study completed in 2010 that identified the barriers to help-seeking in mental health:

1. Public, perceived, and self-stigmatizing attitudes to mental illness

2. Confidentiality and trust

3. Difficulty identifying the symptoms of mental illness

4. Concern about the characteristics of the provider

5. Reliance on self, do not want help

6. Knowledge about mental health services

7. Fear or stress about the act of help-seeking or the source of help itself

8. Lack of accessibility (time, transportation, costs, etc.)

9. Difficulty or unwillingness to express emotions

10. Do not want to burden someone else

11. Prefer other sources of help (family, friends, etc.)

12. Worry about effect on career

13. Others not recognizing the need for help or not having the skills to cope

The same study also identified factors that made it more likely that someone would engage in help seeking:

1. Positive past experience with help-seeking

2. Social support or encouragement from others

3. Confidentiality and trust in the provider

4. Positive relationship with service staff

5. Education and awareness

6. Perceiving the problem as serious

7. Ease of expressing emotions and openness

8. Positive attitudes toward seeking help

Gulliver, A., Griffiths, K.M., and Christensen, H. (2010). Perceived barriers and facilitators to mental health health seeking in young people. *BMC Psychiatry*, 10, 113.

In addition to all of these factors, additional sources of variance in help-seeking is found among women and men, people with disabilities, persons who are hard of hearing or deaf, persons of color, particular ethnic groups, and age factors (consider the generations discussed in Chapter 9...which generations do you think are more apt to seek help? Which of these would be potential barriers or facilitators to you seeking help?).

Treatment and Rehabilitation

It is not common for a book to make a distinction between treatment and rehabilitation in mental health. My experience has been that it is a critical distinction between different providers of services within the mental health field. This distinction also applies in other fields such as physical, occupational, and speech therapy.

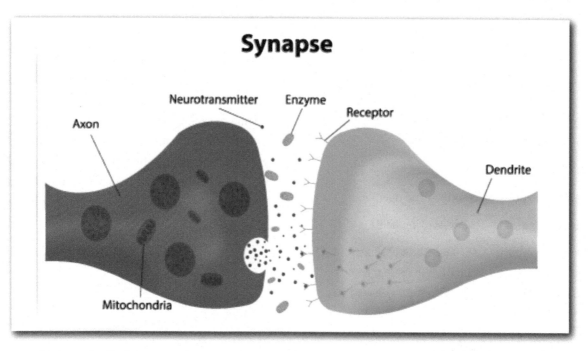

Synapse

Axon

Neurotransmitter

Enzyme

Receptor

Dendrite

Mitochondria

This image details the presence of neurotransmitters in the synaptic gap that activate or deactivate the adjacent cell. Psychotropic medications are designed to mimic specific neurotransmitters or impact the level of neurotransmitters in the synaptic gap.

These medications impact the targeted areas of the brain that are problematic, but also interfere with neurological transmission throughout the body...thus, these medications are as well known for their "side effects" as their "therapeutic effects."

Treatment

We know from Chapter 15 that a specific mental health problem has symptoms. These are the aspects of the experience that we find unpleasant (they are also rare, in violation of a social norm, and/or interfere with our functioning).

The focus of **treatment** is to reduce or eliminate the symptoms of the disorder. Successful treatment of depression means that symptoms of depression, such as lack of energy, difficulty with sleeping/eating, lethargy, and suicidal ideation are reduced in frequency/intensity or eliminated all together.

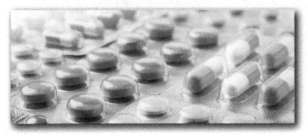

The primary method of addressing treatment for mental disorders is through the use of **psychotropic medications** (i.e. medications that have an impact on our brain chemistry).

To understand how medications work, you will need to recall the information we covered about the synapse in Chapter 3: Biopsychology.

Another method of treating mental disorders is through **neurosurgery**. The truth is, neurosurgery is very rare and usually used as a last resort when medications of all kinds have already failed. In very rare cases, neurosurgery is used to treat severe depression, severe anxiety, and severe obsessive-compulsive disorder.

Other Treatments

Additional targeted treatments include:

1. Deep brain stimulation - electrodes are inserted into the brain to stimulate parts of the brain.

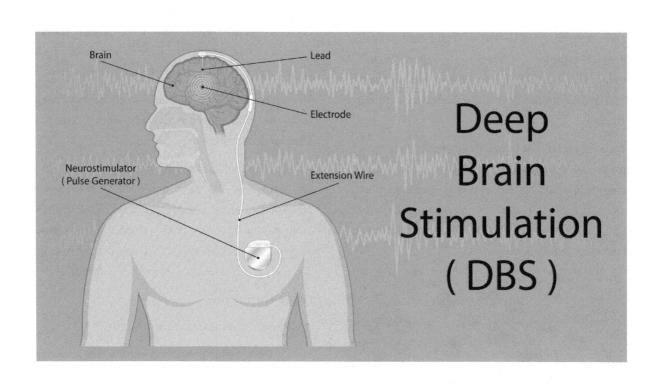

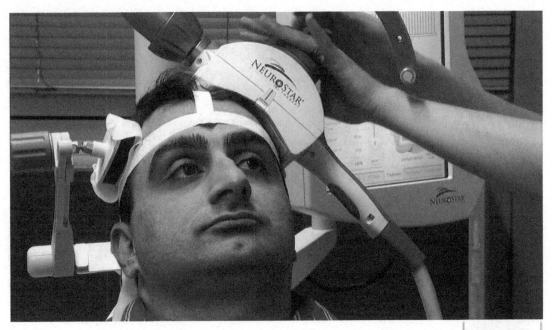

MOVIE - TMS Brain Stimulation can help Combat Depression

MOVIE - The Truth about Electroconvulsive Therapy

2. Vagus verve stimulation - a generator is implanted in the chest and sends electrical stimuli to the vagus nerve in the neck.

3. Electroconvulsive therapy (ECT) - although very controversial, ECT is still used in some cases of severe depression.

Rehabilitation

Rehabilitation technically refers to the process of returning someone to their previous level of functioning or to their maximum functioning, considering their disability. A very clear example of this would be when a person has a stroke. At first, the **treatment** is to arrest the stroke and minimize the damage created by the stroke.

Once a person is stabilized, they are often transferred to a **rehabilitation** facility, where they will engage in physical, occupational, and speech therapy to maximize their functioning. In the end, some damage may be permanent, so the therapies focus on teaching compensatory strategies, using adaptive equipment to increase independence, and modifications of living and working spaces to accommodate for the disability.

Mental health rehabilitation works in much the same way as physical, occupational, and speech therapy. The medications that a client is taking help to reduce or eliminate the symptoms, but the person usually has some additional problems grouped together in the diathesis-stress area of etiology - learning, stress, faulty thinking, and environment.

Psychosocial rehabilitation is a model of rehabilitation specifically designed for persons with chronic, pervasive, and persistent mental illness. Individuals with this level of disability often need case management, support for finances, housing assistance, skill training, and social support because the illness has so devastated their sense of self and opportunities to learn.

Here is a list of the guiding principles for practitioners in the field of psychosocial rehabilitation (PSR):

1. Hope is an essential ingredient in psychosocial rehabilitation. All people have an underutilized capacity to learn and grow that should be developed.

2. All people should be treated with respect and dignity.

3. Service provision strives to meet the client "where they are" and to assist them in moving forward toward their goals.

4. Active participation and choice are the hallmarks of service planning and focus on the stated goals of the person receiving services.

5. PSR focuses on "real world" everyday activities and facilitates the development of skills and supports for people to participate as fully as possible in normal roles within family and community settings.

6. Assumption that persons who receive services have skills, talents, and qualities that can be leveraged to assist the person in the rehabilitative process.

7. Multicultural diversity among PSR program staff, participants, and the community at large is appreciated as a source of strength and program enrichment. Programs take active measures to respond in ways that are considerate and respectful.

8. PSR is premised on self-determination and empowerment.

9. An individualized approach to the development and provision of PSR services best meets the needs of people who choose to use these services.

10. PSR practitioner role is intentionally informal and participatory in activities that are designed

to engage the person with mental illness and cognitive disabilities in the real world.

11. The prevention of unnecessary hospitalizations and the stabilization of community tenure are primary goals of PSR.

Counseling and Psychotherapy

Along with treatment and rehabilitation, we often encounter helping professionals that offer counseling or psychotherapy services. These services, commonly referred to as "talk therapies" endeavor to enhance people's lives through a combination of treatment and rehabilitation activities.

Counseling and psychotherapy are also provided to individuals who do not have mental illness, but have challenges, frustrations, need help problem solving, want to create better habits, or simply want a person to talk to every week. Counseling is a great way to explore issues such as critical decision making, relationships, personal habits, and career planning.

Freud's famous couch - one of the most iconic images portraying Freud's particular brand of therapy.

There are a great number of counseling theories and applications. Some counseling theories focus on processing feelings or behaviors, or reframing traumatic experiences. Some counseling applications include individuals, families, couples, and groups. Check out the link below for a fairly comprehensive list of different therapies and applications.

WIKIPEDIA - List of Psychotherapies

Assessment

Chapter 16 Discussion - Help-Seeking

Review the content on the barriers that exist for people to seek help, including counseling and psychotherapy. If you want, share instances in which you did or did not seek help and the consequences of these decisions.

Chapter 16 Quiz

1. Describe the distinction between treatment and rehabilitation.

Chapter 16 Assignment - Mental Illness

Purpose

The purpose of this assignment is to examine the etiology and treatment of a specific mental illness and present the material to peers. This is modeled after the tradition of poster presentations that are an integral part of the decimation of new knowledge in the field of psychology.

Creating visually appealing images coupled with informative text also allows students to exercise creativity and artistry in an academic setting. These skills are useful for all matter of presentations in a professional life.

Skills and Knowledge

You will demonstrate the following skills and knowledge by completing this assignment:

1. Research details related to a specific mental illness.

2. Collect data from numerous sources regarding mental illness, diagnostic criteria, etiology, and treatment options.

3. Present data in a visually appealing, graphic-intensive format (infographic).

Task

To start, you will revisit the site mentioned in Chapter 15.

Mental Health Conditions - NAMI

Your instructor may assign you a specific mental health condition, or you can negotiate one of your choice.

Your task is to research the diagnostic criteria (from the source above, but also from the DSM-5), the etiology of the diagnosis, and treatments for the symptoms.

This information will be visually organized in an infographic and will be displayed in the classroom, where students will be expected to explain their infographic to the other members of the class and to some potential visitors (for face-to-face classes).

How to Create an Infographic

Infographics are accessible and interesting ways to present information in a colorful and graphically intensive manner.

One of the best tools I have used is called Canva. It is available on the web and as an iOS or Android app. Canva will always try to get you to upgrade to the pro version, but you can do fine work with the free version.

Check out www.canva.com

1. Sign up for a FREE student account.

2. This will give you access to a huge number of templates.

3. Play around with different designs that fit with your topic.

4. You can replace the graphic elements with your own.

Canva App for iOS

Canva App for Android

Criteria for Success

Use the rubric below as a guide to this assignment:

Infographic   10 points

Presentation has been developed to portray an infographic.

Diagnosis   20 points

The accurate name and diagnostic criteria for the disorder.

Etiology   10 points

Causes, both biological and psychosocial are presented.

Treatments   20 points

Treatments, biological (medications), rehabilitation, and therapy are discussed.

Poster Organization   20 points

The information on the poster is well organized and clear.

Graphics   10 points

Graphic elements are appropriate to the topic and helpful in understanding information.

Mechanics   10 points

Layout, use of space, color, fonts, and professionalism.

In addition, I would like you to post a link to your infographic in the discussion board called "Chapter 16 Assignment Infographic." This is voluntary and not graded.

Special
Assignments

Correlation

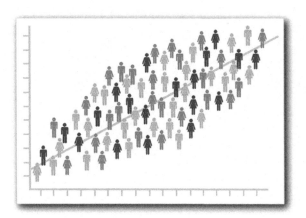

Purpose

The purpose of this assignment is to have you experience making a decision based upon statistical data that you calculate from a set of data. This is precisely what psychologists do in their research. Despite our preconceptions (and even despite our hypotheses) we must let the data determine the answer to our question. Sometimes these answers are hard to understand or even believe, but that is the wonder of the field of psychology.

While this assignment provides a data set for you to use, your instructor may elect to have you perform actual data collection instead. You would then create an Excel file similar to the one provided and complete the assignment following the same instructions.

Skills and Knowledge

You will demonstrate the following skills and knowledge by completing this assignment:

1. Construct a spreadsheet of data.

2. Construct appropriate hypotheses.

3. Using the tools within the spreadsheet, calculate the correlation coefficient of the data.

4. Report the statistical results and meaning.

5. Draw conclusions about each of your hypotheses.

Task

Company X primarily uses two techniques to evaluate job applicants: (a) intelligence as measured by a standard IQ scale, and (b) a formal interview in which they are judged on a 1 (Poor) to 7 (Excellent) scale.

An industrial-organizational psychologist working for Company X is interested in investigating the validity of this selection process. To do so, he collects data from the personnel files of 17 employees hired during 2007.

He records their IQ score, interview score, and the result of their 1-year performance review, in which their work performance was assessed on a scale from 0 (Very Poor) to 10 (Very Good).

Set up the Assignment in Excel

To complete this assignment, you will need to use Microsoft Excel. You can use this software on your iPad or any other computer you have access to.

iPad version of MS Excel

Tap the icon to download Excel for iPad

1. Create a spreadsheet in Microsoft Excel (or another spreadsheet; however, the assignment is designed to support Microsoft Excel).

2. Enter the data from the following table.

IQ	Interview	Performance
103	7	5
119	5	9
100	4	7
103	7	6
112	5	9
129	6	10
89	6	7
99	6	5
84	7	7
104	4	7
89	4	8
132	6	8
87	4	7
109	4	9
139	5	10
93	2	7
83	5	5

Create your Hypotheses

Now, consider the data. You have been given IQ scores, interview scores, and performance scores. Could knowing one of these scores predict the others? That is the purpose of calculating the correlation! Consider these relationships and write an hypothesis about each one.

An hypothesis is a "guess" as to how you think the relationship will play out when you do the statistics. It is your guess on the type of relationship that will exist between the two variables.

In this study, we can examine three relationships between the variables:

- The relationship between IQ and performance scores

- The relationship between interview scores and performance scores

- The relationship between IQ and interview scores

Based on your personal experience (in a real study we would base this on the current knowledge in the field), what do you think these correlations are going to look like?

Consider what you have already learned about correlations. They simply describe that when one number goes up, the other goes up (positive # correlations) and when one number goes up, the other goes down (negative # correlations).

Look at each of our relationships...will high IQ people also have high performance? Will high interview scores go along with high performance? Do people with high IQ do better in interviews?

To write out a set of hypotheses you have to predict a relationship. You then have to have an accompanying hypothesis that says there is NO RELATIONSHIP (null hypothesis). The data will support ONE of each of these hypotheses.

If you thought that people with high IQ would NOT perform better in interviews (thus low interview scores), then you might write your hypotheses like this:

H1 (experimental hypothesis) - Persons with high IQ scores will perform less well in interviews than those with low IQs.

H0 (null hypothesis) - There will be no relationship between IQ scores and interview scores.

Your three different hypotheses (one for each relationship) should look a lot like the examples above.

This is how science works...we propose experimental hypotheses and then collect and analyze data to see if the data supports it. If it does NOT support it, then the data supports the NULL hypothesis. So there is ALWAYS an hypothesis that is supported, either the experimental (H1) or the null (H0).

Calculate the Three Correlations

Now you are ready to compute the correlation.

Calculating a Correlation in Excel

Select a cell on the sheet for each of the correlations you are calculating and label them:

- IQ-vs-Performance
- Interview-vs-Performance
- IQ-vs-Interview

Check your Hypotheses

Now that you have your correlations for each hypothesized relationship, write three statements, one for each, as to what you can conclude about the relationship between each set of variables.

Submission

All of the information outlined in the following rubric is contained in the first sheet of your spreadsheet. You will be uploading a copy of the spreadsheet itself to the drop box.

Criteria for Success

Your assignment will be graded using the following rubric:

Excel File   10 points

The file that is submitted is an Excel file or equivalent spreadsheet file.

Name   10 points

Your name is included in the document.

Data   10 points

Data is copied into the sheet.

Hypotheses   20 points

You have listed your hypothesis for each of the three relationships.

Calculation of Correlation   20 points

Correct correlations for all three relationships.

Decision on Hypotheses   30 points

A single statement regarding each hypothesis is included.

Based on a different set of data, I completed this assignment. Your spreadsheet should look very much like the image below, with the exception that you are going to reporting out on three different hypotheses using three different correlations.

The study below shows subjects' height and the time it took for them to run a specific distance. I wanted to find out if height was related to speed (keeping in mind that lower times mean faster speeds.)

The correlation was very strong (-.98) so height really does impact running speed. Taller people are faster.

	A	B	C	D	E
1	HEIGHT	TIME			
2	60	8		Hypothesis	Increased hight will result in lower times
3	55	11		Height-Time	-0.976152211
4	56	10			
5	52	12		Statement	My hypthesis was correct, taller people ran faster, therefore their times would be lower.
6	48	14			
7	44	16			
8	47	13			
9	52	12			
10					
11	Mark H. Kavanaugh				
12					
13					

Personal Change

Purpose

The purpose of this assignment is to utilize the knowledge gained in the study of operant conditioning to bring about a positive personal change in your life. As a theory of psychology, behaviorism is one of the most respected and effective approaches to change.

Nearly every self-help system utilizes the essential factors associated with operant conditioning. The video game and gambling worlds have capitalized on these principles to keep people playing. Using the same techniques, educators "gamify" their content to encourage learning and to get their students "addicted" to the course!

Skills and Knowledge

You will demonstrate the following skills and knowledge by completing this assignment:

1. Identify an area of personal change that you wish to address.

2. Determine the difference between applications of operant conditioning when you are trying to add/increase a behavior, versus when you are trying to eliminate/decrease a behavior.

3. Identify a reasonable rate of behavior change given the time frame for the project.

4. Identify potential reinforcers to be used in the behavior plan.

5. Write a behavior plan accurately describing the behavior when the Dead Man and Stranger Tests are applied.

6. Implement that plan and maintain accurate records.

7. Evaluate the plan and suggest changes to the plan that would make it more effective.

Task

In this course, you are learning about the most powerful and successful methods for bringing about behavior change in yourself or others. While it may seem common sense, there is a deep science that dictates how these methods are most successfully applied.

For this project, you are going to identify a specific behavior that you would like to add/increase or eliminate/decrease in your life. For instance, you may want to add/increase your exercise routine or, conversely, you may want to eliminate/reduce your intake of sweets.

The ABC Contingency Theory

As described in Chapter 6, you will be applying the ABC contingency theory to to manipulate the antecedents and consequences that operate on your target behavior.

You would be wise to re-read the material from Chapter 6 to re-familiarize yourself with these concepts.

Please review the resources from Chapter 6!

Adding or Increasing Works Better

One fact about operant conditioning is that it is much easier (and more effective) to identify a behavior that you want to add/increase than one you want to eliminate/decrease. To take advantage of this fact, we will focus this project solely on adding/increasing behaviors.

If your goal is to eliminate/decrease a behavior, you will work with your teacher to identify an "incompatible behavior" (something that you are going to do INSTEAD of the target behavior, and develop a plan to choose THAT behavior instead).

Describing your Behavior

One of the key factors for operant conditioning is defining the behavior that you want to add/increase in very specific, "measurable" terms. In order to help with this, there are two "tests" that you can use to evaluate the statement of your behavior...the Dead Man Test and the Stranger Test.

Dead Man Test

The implication of the Dead Man Test is that IF a dead man can be observed "doing" the behavior, then your description FAILS and you need to rewrite it. Here are some examples:

"Sally will sit quietly."

"Bob will not hit his little brother."

"Roberta will not longer order large Starbucks drinks."

Consider these for a moment...if you do, you can see that, in fact, you can prop up a "dead man" and they can "do" these things! A dead man can sit quietly, and a dead man can NOT hit his little brother, and will NOT order drinks!

The Dead Man's Test eliminates all the "shall not" types of behavior plans. Here are some alternatives that pass the Dead Man's Test:

"Sally will sit at her desk and complete 2 worksheets in the next hour."

"When Bob feels like hitting his brother, he will go to his room and use his punching bag for 3 minutes."

"Roberta will order small juice or coffee drinks at Starbucks."

Stranger Test

The Stranger Test makes sure that the behavior description is measurable. Essentially, when you apply the Stranger Test you ask if a stranger (someone who does not know you) would be able to identify when the behavior happens. This keeps us from using our own personal terms to describe behavior, and it allows us to keep records for when the behavior did and did not happen.

Consider these examples:

"Instead of throwing a fit, Stan will hug his "Bunky.""

"Lucy will be nice to her classmates."

"Mark will go to the gym."

Again, consider a stranger looking at these descriptions. People who know Stan might know what his "fits" look like and they might know that "Bunky" is his favorite stuffed toy, but a stranger would not. What does "nice" mean for Lucy? Finally, technically Mark can go to the gym, but if he just walked over there and stood inside for a minute, that is really not what we are looking for! Each of these fails the Stranger Test!

Here are some alternatives that pass the Stranger Test:

"When Stan feels he wants to throw his school supplies on the floor, he will stand up, go to the back of the room, and sit in the chair with is comfort toy named "Bunky.""

"When Lucy is in class, she will not take other students' art supplies without first asking to borrow them and receiving a confirmation that it is OK."

"Mark will go to the gym 3 times a week and engage in 1/2 hour of cardio training on the treadmill and swim a total of 5 laps in the pool."

Identifying Reinforcers

Operant conditioning works when we make specific rewards accessible when we have achieved our target behavior. Selecting reinforcers, and withholding them unless you complete your goal, is the key part of personal change planning.

A reinforcer can be anything that you want or anything that you already have and enjoy. It can also be an activity that you enjoy a lot (even just watching TV!). The difference is that NOW that it is part of a plan, you need to EARN it!

It is recommended that you work with your teacher to identify multiple possible reinforcers.

Plan Statement

The plan statement in a behavior plan is a single line that outlines the entirety of the plan in a single sentence (although it can be done in more than one sentence). It includes the where/when of the behavior, a description of the behavior, and the rate of success needed to get the reinforcer. Here is an example:

"Each week, Mark will go to the gym 3 separate days and engage in 1/2 hour of cardio and swim 5 laps. Each week Mark succeeds in performing this task, he will allow himself to purchase one movie ticket for the weekend."

Steps in the Process

Here are the steps to completing this project:

1. Identify the target behavior, where/when the behavior occurs, and your target goal for that behavior.

2. Record the current rate of this behavior. If it is a new behavior, the current rate would be zero.

3. Identify potential reinforcers that you will withhold in order to use them in your plan.

4. Compose the plan statement that encompasses an identification of where/when the behavior

will occur, the actual description of the behavior (passing both the Dead Man and Stranger Tests) and the degree of performance that will bring about the reinforcer, and an identification of the reinforcer.

5. Implement the plan for at least 4 weeks.

6. Track the behavior and the success of the plan (when reinforcers were earned).

7. After the implementation period, evaluate the record that you have and reflect on the relative success or failure of the plan, making suggestions for changes or improvements.

Criteria for Success

Your assignment will be graded using the following rubric:

Title Page   10 points
Standard title page with name, date, course, college name and the name of the assignment.

Target Behavior   10 points
This is a statement of the goal that you have in your own words. It does not have to pass the tests yet.

Baseline   10 points
Provide a statement that reflects the current rate of this behavior.

Reinforcers   10 points
Identify at least two separate reinforcers that you can use in this plan.

Plan Statement   10 points
A concise statement of the plan.

Dead Man's Test   10 points
The statement passes the Dead Man's Test.

Stranger Test   10 points
The statement passes the Stranger Test.

Record of Implementation   10 points
A table in included that shows the data collected during the implementation period.

Evaluation   10 points
A statement is made as to if the plan worked or not. Additional statements are made about how the plan could be changed or improved.

Mechanics   10 points

Spelling, syntax, and organizational structure of the paper. Clear and organized.

Information Literacy Paper (ILP)

Purpose

The purpose of this assignment is to discover, read, understand, and communicate a summary information related to recent research within the social sciences.

By exploring peer-reviewed resources of data, you will better appreciate the depth of knowledge and contribution of social sciences to our human knowledge.

Fundamentally, this assignment is also to provide an opportunity for you to develop appropriate research questions, access peer-reviewed literature, and to write in an expository, scientific way.

Skills and Knowledge

You will demonstrate the following skills and knowledge by completing this assignment:

1. Available peer-reviewed resources related to social sciences.

2. Specific applications (depending upon your research question) of this data to real-world problem solving.

3. Modern methods of research and data collection in the field of social sciences.

4. The development of an appropriate research question in the field of social sciences.

5. Locating and reviewing peer reviewed literature.

6. Identifying sources relevant to answering your research question.

7. Summarizing your findings from peer-reviewed resources.

8. Writing an academic paper organized with an introduction, a review of the relevant literature, and a conclusion.

9. Formatting an academic paper in accordance to the American Psychological Associations (APA) writing standards.

10. Utilizing feedback received on specific parts of the assignment to improve personal performance.

Task

This project is broken down into four parts. While only the Final Submission will be used to calculate your grade, each part is REQUIRED.

Part I - Asking a Good Question

Part II - Sources and APA Style

Part III - Draft Submission

Part IV - Final Submission

Image from library.albion.edu

ILP Part I - Asking Good Questions

The difference between a research paper and other forms of writing is apparent within the definition of a Research Paper.

A research paper is a document that explores the knowledge that is available within a particular field of study and presents that knowledge in the effort to answer a particular research question.

The point is that you are looking at a body of knowledge in a field, such as psychology, sociology, or communication, and you are trying to find out what we already know about the question you have. How you phrase that question is key to getting at the right information!

Coming up with Questions

There are all sorts of interesting things to think about in the social sciences...really, social sciences deal with everyday life and the extremes of human behavior.

However, we have been at this for quite some time so some of the basic questions such as "What is abnormal?", or "How do people communicate?", or even, "What is Schizophrenia?" have been written about enough and the answers to these questions are either easy to find with simple searchers or they are very complex and beyond the scope of a research paper.

You want to focus you paper on a very specific question that is important to you...that will not only narrow down your search for answers, but it will also motivate you to do the paper.

Focus, Focus, Focus

Good research try to answer "real" questions...not just definitions like you might do in an expository paper. Since so much research has already been done you have to narrow your topic and focus your research.

Examples:

Here are some examples of how you transform an interesting TOPIC into a researchable QUESTION

TOPIC: Differences between the genders in communication

RESEARCHABLE QUESTION: What strategies can couples use to mitigate the different styles of communication between men and women?

RESEARCHABLE QUESTION: How do men and women's communication styles differ in the context of a Muslim community?

RESEARCHABLE QUESTION: How do men and women interpret "assertiveness" and "aggressiveness" in interpersonal communication?

TOPIC: Autism

RESEARCHABLE QUESTION: Which behavior modification techniques are best for use with a child with moderate Autism in the home?

RESEARCHABLE QUESTION: How effective have wilderness therapy programs been when working with teenagers with Autism?

TOPIC: Religion or prayer or meditation

RESEARCHABLE QUESTION: What are the potential physiological benefits of deep prayer and/or meditation?

RESEARCHABLE QUESTION: What is the relationship between religious belief and happiness in marriage?

Finding your Question

As you can see...these questions are MUCH more precise and they answer REAL WORLD questions!

Your task is to move from TOPIC to RESEARCHABLE QUESTION

Sometimes you need to go ahead and begin searching on Google or within the Online Databases to find out what may be interesting to study! You can just search Google using the terms from the course and see what you find on the web. Although you will not be using the web as a primary source, often the articles and posts on the web contain information about the scientists that are doing the work you are interested in. You can then look up these names in the online databases related to your topics

Psychology Topics

These instructions are generic to social sciences so the following sources can often be used for any social science class. These are also great resources for questions you may explore for research papers in other classes.

Visit the APS website!

If you go to this website and click on the Research Topics link, you can review all sorts of the latest topics being researched in Psychology. This should inspire you to look into topics that you find interesting!

100 Sociology Research Topics

Controversial questions also make for great research. Here are links to a document that lists a great number of controversial topics related to social sciences.

Controversial Topics (MS Word)

Controversial Topics (PDF)

ILP Proposal

Find the quiz titled ILP Proposal.

This Quiz is made up of the following two questions:

1. State your research question. (Remember, the question must be in the form of a QUESTION, not a statement.)

2. Describe why you are interested in this particular question.

This quiz serves as a communication tool between you and your instructor. Your instructor will grade these two questions and provide feedback. Your goal is to get a score of 100 on this quiz, that will mean that the research question has been approved. You may have to take this quiz a number of times, correcting your answers based on the feedback you get from your instructor. Keep taking the quiz until you get a score of 100, but be sure to review your instructor's feedback even if you DO score a 100.

Papers submitted without this process being complete may not be accepted.

Part II - Sources and APA Style

Evaluating Information

In a world full of information at our fingertips, it is that much more important to evaluate the source of our data and information. It is easy for nearly anyone to publish ideas. While this has certainly democratized the world of data, it has brought on a lot of challenges including everything from students using Wikipedia to do research and "Fake News".

At all times, when you encounter information, you should evaluate the SOURCE of that information.

Click HERE to view a valuable set of tips for evaluating information you find in print and on the web published by the library at the University of Alaska Fairbanks.

Limits on the Data you will Access

For the purpose of this assignment you are going to use a very limited set of resources. You are essentially going to be doing a report on what experts in the field have to say about your topic. As such you are ONLY going to report from peer reviewed research articles and professional websites.

This does not mean that you can't use Google and other search engines. In fact, I use them all the time. I use Google to find out the basic information, names, and terms for my question and then I apply these terms to my searches in the library databases.

Peer Reviewed Articles

Peer Reviewed Article is an article that has been reviewed by others in the field for accuracy and good methodology

1. You won't find these at Barnes and Noble

2. These articles tend to appear in special publications called "Journals"

3. Nearly every field has a Journal of some kind where the latest research in the field is reported to others who are professionals and also interested in the field

4. Here is a VERY small list of some of the journals from the field of Sociology:

   1. American Sociological Review

   2. Sociology of Education

   3. Society and Mental Health

   4. Journal of Marriage and Family

If we were to look up information on "communication between men and women", here is an example of a typical peer reviewed article:

Junco, R., Merson, D., & Salter, D. W. (2010). The effect of gender, ethnicity, and income on college students' use of communication technologies. CyberPsychology, Behavior & Social Networking, 13(6), 619-627.

Finding Peer Reviewed Articles

The library is your source for access to peer reviewed journal articles on your topic. library staff can assist you in the following ways:

1. Focusing your research topic or area.

2. Assisting in finding the best search terms to use in the online databases.

3. Using the database settings to focus your research on peer-reviewed, full-text, recent articles.

4. Assisting you in getting additional materials which may not be in the databases.

The information that you are going to include in your paper to answer your question is going to come **exclusively** from peer reviewed articles and professional websites. Please use the resources at the library to meet these objectives.

Accessing Library Resources

As part of this assignment you should attend a Library Orientation meeting (face-to-face or virtual) to learn about the resources available at our local academic library.

While there are a number of different sources of peer-reviewed articles, this assignment limits your search to those databases supported by our library. In addition, you will be required to access assistance from library staff to use the databases and/or access materials outside of the databases.

This assignment will document your search process, utilization of library resources and your ability to construct a references page.

APA Writing Style

The American Psychological Association produces a publishing manual which outlines the expectations for all aspects of formatting a paper for publication. In undergraduate work, the typical expectations are not as stringent, but are important to learn.

While the details of formatting a paper, title pages, references, and in-text citations may seem cumbersome, the format assures that all writers are provides the same formatting instructions and it serves to prevent plagiarism.

APA Formatting Poster from Purdue University

While the best way to learn APA format is to purchase the APA Publishing Guide, Purdue University publishes a very popular Online Writing Lab with ample services to assist you in learning how to write in APA style.

APA Formatting and Style Guide

Writing your Paper

Once you have read all your articles, taken notes, and put your thoughts together, you want to sit and write your paper. Communicating in writing is one of the most important skills you are going to develop in college. Some of you may already be good writers, others may have to work hard to build on existing skills. I'm going to give you some writing tips here, along with some expectations for formatting your paper so that it is acceptable as a Psychology academic paper.

Academic Voice and the Format of your Paper

At this level of your academic career you are beginning to develop the voice you will have that you will use, in both writing and speaking, to influence others. How you communicate is just as important as what you communicate. Some of the best ideas have fallen to the sidelines because they were not communicated well (sadly, some really bad ideas have also seen the light of day because of the eloquence with which they were communicated!)

Writing in an Academic Way

As you are taking notes and beginning to put together your paper, keep the above graphic in mind:

1. **Be critical and analytical** - Don't take everything on face value, think about what you are reading and if it makes sense. How does it fit in with the research question of your paper?

2. **Make use of subject specific language** - Are there specific terms being used in the articles that you are reading? Use them! However, don't try to write so you "sound" smart, use your natural writing style but include the specific language for the field.

3. **Being precise in meaning** - Think clearly about what you are trying to say in each paragraph, each sentence. Is it clear? Can anyone understand what you are saying? Have others read and tell you what they think it means.

4. **Citing sources to support your position** - You are not an expert in this field (not yet!) So, you really can't make statements without having some sort of evidence to back it up! Your arti-

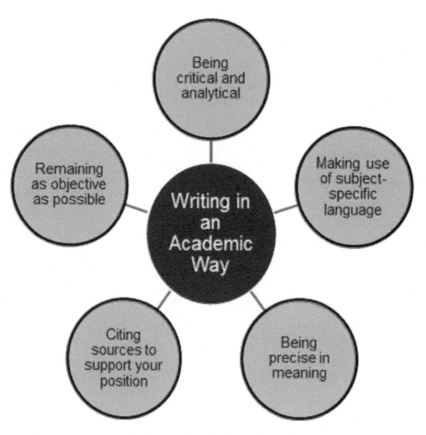

Image from **advantagelearningcenter.com**

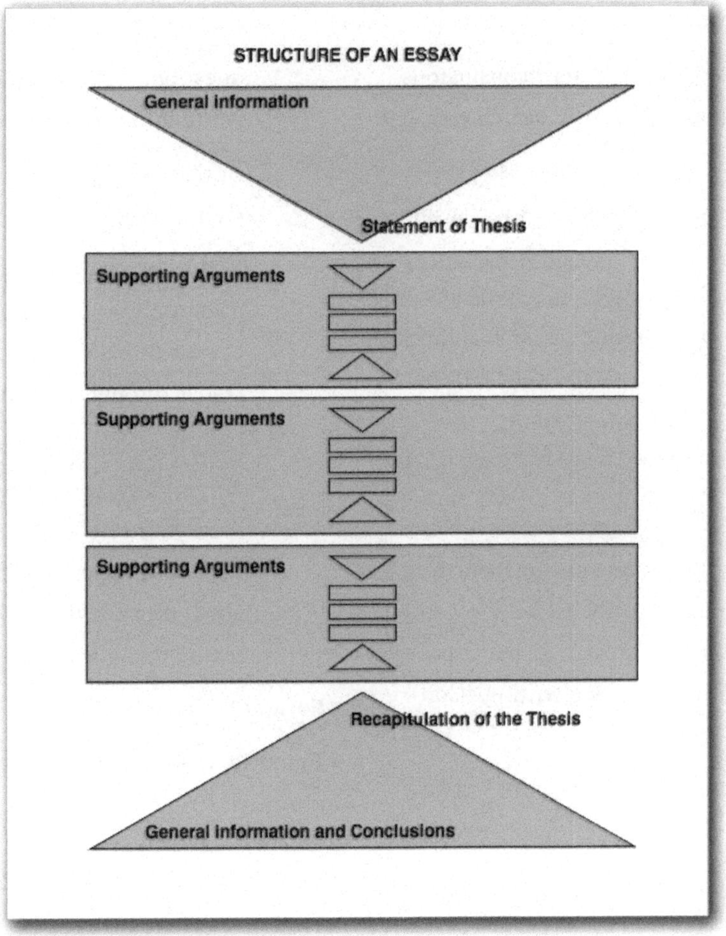

STRUCTURE OF AN ESSAY

General information

Statement of Thesis

Supporting Arguments

Supporting Arguments

Supporting Arguments

Recapitulation of the Thesis

General information and Conclusions

cles are this evidence. Do not draw conclusions that cannot be supported by the research you have found.

5. **Remain as objective as possible** - You may go into a topic with your mind already made up. This is called bias. That is OK, but you need to set it aside while you are doing research and be open to other points of view. You need to report the facts...everyone has the right to their opinion but we don't have the right to our own facts!

Flow of your Writing

Another component of writing is how the introduction, supporting paragraphs, and conclusion all work together. There is a certain amount of "breathing" that a paper does that makes good writing into great writing. Consider this graphic.

1. Note how the introduction starts with general statements about the context of the research question...guide your audience from the larger world into your specific question.

2. At the end of the introduction you should state your question.

3. Each supporting paragraph (these could be pages or even chapters) is also structured like the whole paper with guiding points to lead your reader through your information.

4. Start the conclusion by bringing your reader's attention back to the research question. Move out from your research question into a summary of the whole paper and then general conclusions about how the research is important in the context of the larger world.

Formal Writing Formats

(no...APA does not stand for Advocates for Porcupines of America)

Since the primary product of Psychological research is writing, the American Psychological Association took upon itself to outline specific writing conventions and practices so that information can be presented in a consistent and easy to understand manner. Resources on writing in APA Format can be found in the Appendix of this CourseBook.

ILP Part III - Draft Submission

A Draft Submission is Required

Your draft will attempt to meet all of the criteria of your Final Submission (see below.) This draft is an opportunity for you to receive feedback on your format, the structure of your paper, your use of peer-reviewed literature, and a review of your introduction and conclusion sections.

It is expected that you will revise this draft upon receipt of this feedback prior to your Final Submission.

ILP Part IV - Final Submission

One you have obtained your feedback from the draft submission, rewrite your paper and submit your final draft.

ILP Final Submission

Find the assignment titled ILP Final Submission. Submit your final paper to to this drop box.

Title Page   5 points

Paper includes a title page (name, date, assignment name, class, school) that is the first page of a single document. Paper is formatted clearly and organized. Paper is in the correct file format of MS Word or PDF

Introduction   5 points

The introduction is written in such a way as to allow the reader to move into the subject of the paper gradually. The author introduces a broader perspective first and then brings the reader in closer to reveal the research question.

Introduction   5 points

While not covering the articles at all, the author provides a very brief glimpse as to the scope and content of the research that is going to be discussed in the paper.

Introduction   10 points

The research question is stated clearly and in a question format.

Literature Review   10 points

The bulk of the data covered in the body of the is from peer-reviewed sources.

Literature Review   10 points

The presentation of information from the sources is logical and follows a straightforward line of reasoning to draw conclusions at the end.

Literature Review   10 points

All sources are cited appropriately using in-text citations that correspond with resources listed in the references.

Conclusion   5 points

Author restates the purpose of the paper/the research question.

Conclusion   10 points

There is a brief summary of the information that was presented in the paper and this summary is followed by logical conclusions.

Conclusion   5 points

The research question is stated clearly and in a question format.

References   5 points

References start on a new page...the last page(s) of the document.

References   10 points

APA Style references - Hanging indent, double spaced, no extra space between citations, correct format of all aspects of the citation.

Mechanics   10 points

Spelling, syntax, and organizational structure of the paper. Clear

Made in the USA
Las Vegas, NV
08 August 2022

52904787R00234